The COOKS' Book

The COOKS' Book

FOR THE COOK WHO'S

Best AT Everything

LOUISE DIXON

Hardie Grant Books

Published in 2008 by
Hardie Grant Books
85 High Street
Prahran, Victoria 3181, Australia
www.hardiegrant.com.au

First published in the United Kingdom in 2008 by
Michael O'Mara Books Limited
9 Lion Yard, Tremadoc Road
London SW4 7NQ

Cataloguing-in-Publication data is available from the
National Library of Australia.

ISBN 978 1 74066 690 9

Cover image and illustrations © David Woodroffe 2008 except those
on pages 10, 13, 14, 15, 21, 23, 24, 31, 33, 37, 85, 95, 99, 103, 149

Cover design by Ana Bjezancevic from an original design by
www.blacksheep-uk.com

Designed and typeset by Martin Bristow

Printed and bound in England by Clays Ltd, St Ives plc

1 3 5 7 9 10 8 6 4 2

For my mother-in-law, with love

Contents

CONTENTS

Introduction

If you are interested in cooking and food, you probably have lots of recipe books that you refer to time after time, tried and tested dishes that you like cooking and enjoy serving to friends and family. *The Cooks' Book* looks at cooking from a different angle. It's not a recipe book (though there are some recipes in it); it's more a book of techniques and tips, some of which are fairly new, others that have served generations of cooks down the ages, all of which are still useful in today's kitchens.

There are a few important things you should think about when choosing and preparing fresh food. Firstly, although the supermarket is cheap and convenient, have a look at where their fresh stock comes from. Of course, if you're buying a tropical fruit or goods that aren't usually found in your area, you're unlikely to find a good local retailer, but if you're after staples like onions, potatoes, green beans, apples, pears and the like, then try to make sure they are grown, picked and prepared in your region, as it means they haven't been picked weeks previously, washed, packed and transported thousands of miles to get to your table. Bear in mind that as soon as vegetables and fruit are picked and packed, they start to lose their nutritional value. The same applies to meat and fish, so the fresher your ingredients, the tastier and more full of goodness they are.

Secondly, spare a thought for your cooking methods. If you haven't steamed your food before, try it – the flavours and texture will be so much better, the nutrients will be preserved – that's what 'getting the most out of your food' really means. If speed's your thing, stir-frying is not only fast, it's healthy too, and your ingredients – meat, fish, vegetables or any combination – will retain their texture and flavour.

Thirdly, enjoy the process of cooking and preparing a meal, even the day-to-day meals you cook for yourself or your family. It's not easy to come up with delicious and original dishes all the time, but cooking fresh ingredients is so much better than slamming something ready-prepared in the oven every night. Making a meal for others is a very special thing to do, too, not only for the food, but for the table setting, the wine you choose, the music you play. The whole experience is meant to be enjoyable, from the food preparation to the final farewells, and the last thing your guests want is for their host to be exhausted when it comes to the main event, so plan your menu with simple but delicious dishes rather than over-complicated extravaganzas.

Intended for everyone who enjoys cooking and experimenting in the kitchen, *The Cooks' Book* is a collection of information, tips, facts, fun and a few recipes and tricks that might help you out in a crisis. Hopefully, it might also inspire you to try some new things and look at the food you buy in a different way. Enjoy!

Kitchen Essentials

There are a number of things that every good cook needs for a well-equipped kitchen. The rule of thumb on all these is: buy the best-quality equipment you can afford. The better the design, the easier the item will be to use and clean – and the longer it will last.

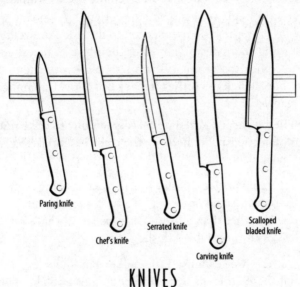

Paring knife

Chef's knife

Serrated knife

Carving knife

Scalloped bladed knife

KNIVES

Quality knives are made from stainless steel with a high carbon content. Best kept in a wooden knife block, there are five basic knives to look for:

* Paring knife – has a short blade and is useful for cutting fruits and vegetables, meat and cheese.

* Chef's knife – this is the longer-bladed knife, the same shape as the paring knife but typically around 20 cm long. Essential for chopping, dicing and mincing.

* Serrated knife – comes in various sizes and will cut bread and cakes evenly.

* Carving knife – essential for the perfect Sunday joint, a carving knife will slice through hot meat effortlessly.

* Scalloped bladed knife – will cut through cold meats better than a carving knife.

PEELERS AND GRATERS

There are many specialized items you can buy to grate nutmeg or Parmesan cheese, but here are the three essentials that you'll call on most often:

* Vegetable peeler – easier to use than a paring knife for potatoes and other veg. Go for a swivel-bladed peeler rather than a fixed-blade, as it will shave off less of the vegetable's flesh.

* Grater – we've all used the hollow box-shaped grater, but there are many more efficient ones available now, including a less messy bowl-shaped version that is easier to use and less tiring on the arms!

* Zester – these have a stainless steel rectangular head with five holes in the top, which you drag down the surface of the fruit to produce fine shavings of citrus zest.

MIXING BOWLS

A well-equipped kitchen will have mixing bowls in different sizes. It's also useful to have a variety of glass, ceramic and stainless steel bowls. Stainless steel bowls are lightweight and good conductors of heat and coldness, while glass and ceramic bowls are heavier and sit more firmly on the worktop while the ingredients are beaten.

WHISKS

There are many different sizes available, from large balloon whisks for whipping cream to small ones used for salad dressings. A good whisk should feel comfortable to hold.

SPOONS

* Wooden spoons – poor conductors of heat, wooden spoons are ideal for beating and creaming.

* Metal or plastic spoons – are great for basting, stirring and mixing.

* Slotted spoons – are useful for lifting and draining foods out of hot liquid or oil and for skimming fat from soups, etc.

* Ladle – used for serving liquids, a ladle with a lip at the side is very useful and makes pouring much easier.

MEASURING SPOONS AND JUGS

All successful cooking is based on the right amounts of ingredients going into the recipe, so make sure you have a set of measuring spoons that graduate from ¼ teaspoon to 1 table-spoon, and at least one measuring jug for judging liquid volumes.

SIEVES AND STRAINERS

Made from metal, plastic or wood, sieves and strainers are used with both wet and dry ingredients and come with different sized mesh. Conical shapes are ideal for straining liquid ingredients into bowls or jars, bowl sieves are better for dry ingredients. A colander makes it easy to drain cooked pasta or vegetables, or wash fruits, etc.

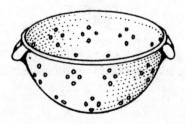

OTHER KITCHEN DEVICES

✳ Food processor – though not absolutely essential, a food processor makes chopping, mincing, dicing and puréeing very easy. Most models come with slicing and shredding attachments as well as dough-making blades.

✳ Blender – really handy for puréeing or liquefying soups, sauces and drinks, a blender isn't as versatile as a food processor, but neither is it as big and bulky.

✳ Mixer – hand-held and worktop mixers are available. They are used for mixing dough, whipping cream, whisking eggs, etc.

✳ Mortar and pestle – small stone or marble bowls with hand-held grinders for grinding spices, nuts and seeds.

✳ Timer – from egg timers to battery-operated, bell-ringing timers, essential for keeping track when preparing trickier recipes.

POTS AND PANS

Three or four saucepans ranging from 1 to 5 litres are all you need for everyday cooking, plus a large two-handled pot for bigger items and stews. But the best thing you could invest in is a good steamer. Steamed foods are not only tastier (because they are cooked so gently), they are also much healthier and retain a greater proportion of the nutrients found in vegetables. Here are a few things to look out for when choosing your pans:

* Select pans that conduct and hold heat evenly, such as cast-iron or aluminium pans.

* Check the weight before you buy. Enamelled cast-iron pans are great to cook with, but they can be very heavy.

* Ensure that the lids fit well and that the handle or knob is secure.

* Make sure the handles are strong and sturdy – and heatproof.

* Check that the bases are thick and heavy.

Cuts of Meat

BEEF

* Shoulder – often labelled 'stewing steak', shoulder is good for slow cooking in stews or casseroles.

* Chuck – again, slow cooking is best with this cut from around the shoulder blades. Often sold cubed for stews, it can also be minced.

* Rib – tender, lean meat and often the source of the traditional roast joint. Should be cooked on the bone. Also the source of rib-eye steaks.

* Sirloin – very tender meat found running from the end of the ribs almost to the end of the back. Source of steaks such as the sirloin, T-bone and fillet and used for roast joints.

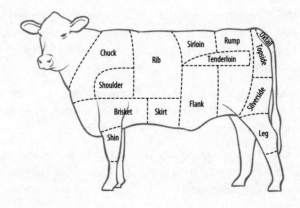

* Tenderloin – found just below the sirloin, the tenderloin can be roasted whole, or cut into tournedos, medallions, filet mignons or Chateaubriand.

* Rump – a good rump steak is said to be the tastiest, but they can be tough and chewy.

* Topside – from the top of the inside leg, topside should be cooked slowly or roasted.

* Silverside – cut from the back of the thigh, silverside is tougher than topside but is very good for marinating.

* Oxtail – very long, slow cooking produces tasty meat and gravy, or, of course, you can make oxtail soup.

* Leg – from the top of the back leg, this meat can be very tough, but braised slowly or pot-roasted, the leg (or hock, as it's also known) is flavoursome.

* Flank – a fatty but tasty cut that is used for mince and corned beef and can be salted.

* Skirt – the name comes from a group of muscles along the flank and inner thighs of the animal. Lean and tasty, skirt meat can be tough, so benefits from slow cooking. Used in steak and kidney pies, corned beef and salted for pastrami.

* Shin – found at the top of the foreleg, this is a cheap cut that benefits from slow cooking. Shin can be braised on the bone or casseroled off the bone.

* Brisket – a tough cut, brisket needs to be cooked slowly and for a long time. Often used for corned beef and salted for pastrami.

LAMB

* Shoulder – quite fatty, but good for roasting and very flavoursome. Can also be boned, rolled and stuffed before roasting.

* Scrag – the part of the neck nearest the head, scrag is best when it's slow-cooked in casseroles.

* Neck – where lamb cutlets come from. The whole joint is called a rack of lamb; two racks make a crown of lamb.

* Loin – where you'll find loin chops. Also, two loins joined together make a saddle of lamb.

* Chump – chump chops are found towards the end of the loin.

* Leg – the traditional roasting cut.

* Shank – usually used for stews and braising.

* Breast – fatty but delicious, the breast is usually served boned, rolled and stuffed.

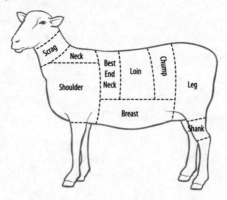

PORK

✳ Shoulder – perfect for roasting, shoulder meat is very succulent.

✳ Loin – again, good for roasting, and also used for loin chops and steaks.

✳ Chump – a cheap cut, chump is good for chops, steaks and escalopes.

✳ Leg – lean meat that is good for roasting, ham and escalopes.

✳ Belly – this is where spare ribs come from. Fatty meat that is good for roasts, sausages, bacon and in stir-fries.

✳ Hand – the tougher and cheaper meat on the animal, usually used for mince and sausages.

✳ Hock – a cheap cut that benefits from being cooked in liquid or slow braising.

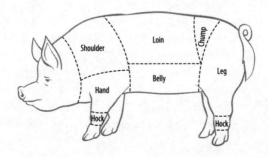

The Food of Love . . .

Cooking can be a chore, or it can be a highly creative and inspiring act – it depends on what you're cooking and for whom you're cooking it. There are certain foods, however, that are prized as libido enhancers, so next time you're preparing a special meal for your loved one, here are ten ingredients that you might bear in mind.

CHOCOLATE

Throughout history, from the ancient Aztec and Mayan civilizations, chocolate has been prized for its aphrodisiacal qualities. In the fifteenth century, it was banned in monasteries in case the consumption of it inflamed the monks. King Louis XV's mistress, Madame du Barry, is said to have made sure her lovers drank a cup of chocolate before allowing them into her bedchamber. The legendary Casanova referred to chocolate as 'the elixir of love'. But they weren't talking about any old chocolate bar one might find in the supermarket, no they were talking about quality goods, with a high cocoa solids content, the type of chocolate that many people quite literally lust after.

There are several reasons why chocolate has such an effect on people. Firstly, its melting point is slightly below human body temperature, so it actually does 'melt in the mouth', a highly sensuous experience in itself. Chocolate also contains serotonin, the body's 'good mood' stimulant, and dopamine, which is the body's natural analgesic. So, chocolate can in fact make you feel uplifted and 'good', maybe this in itself is enough to qualify it as an aphrodisiac?

OYSTERS

The thing about oysters is you either love them or loathe them, and if it's the latter then you are unlikely to find any aphrodisiacal qualities they might hold remotely arousing! Oysters are reputed to look very similar to female genitalia, and it is this similarity that first led people to believe that the oyster could increase one's sexual drive. Good old Casanova was rumoured to eat over fifty raw oysters a day to boost his libido.

Nutritionally, you really can't beat the oyster when it comes to protein and carbohydrate content. They are also a very good source of vitamins A, B, C and D and a host of minerals and omega-3 fatty acids. So although they might not be great to look at, and you might not love the taste, as long as they are properly washed and prepared, the oyster *might* increase your libido and it will definitely make you feel healthy, so it's got to be worth a try.

> *I will not eat oysters. I want my food dead.*
> *Not sick. Not wounded. Dead.*
> **WOODY ALLEN**

ASPARAGUS

The legendary herbalist Nicholas Culpeper noticed that asparagus 'stirs up lust in man and woman'. And, once again, the vitamins and minerals – such as folic acid and potassium – found in the vegetable are not only very beneficial to health, but also produce a general feeling of well-being. The phallic shape of asparagus is also said to lend a certain *je ne sais quoi* to the vegetable . . .

FENNEL

The ancient Egyptians used fennel for its aphrodisiacal qualities, and it is known to be a good source of natural plant oestrogens, which mimic the female sex hormone. Indeed herbalist Nicholas Culpeper recommended a cup of fennel tea per day to stimulate milk production in breastfeeding mothers. Also, in India, roasted fennel seeds are chewed after eating to prevent halitosis – which has to help.

TRUFFLES

Said to make women more tender and men more amiable, the musky scent of the truffle is able to drive some people wild. Indeed, according to the French gastronome, Jean Brillat-Savarin, 'Whoever says "truffle" utters a great word which arouses erotic and gastronomic memories.'

STRAWBERRIES

Always portrayed in art and folklore as sensuous, potent berries that conjure up earthly pleasures and desires, strawberries contain more vitamin C than any other berry, along with good amounts of potassium, folic acid and other vitamins and minerals essential to boosting well-being. Added to that, they are seen as aphrodisiacs because of their large number of seeds, which symbolize fertility.

> *I'm at the age where food has taken the place of sex in my life. In fact, I've just had a mirror put over my kitchen table.*
>
> **RODNEY DANGERFIELD**

BANANAS

It's not just the banana's phallic shape that gets this fruit into the aphrodisiac top ten. This versatile and much-loved food is packed with potassium, magnesium and other important vitamins and minerals that are said to enhance the libido. In Hindu culture, bananas are hailed as a symbol of fertility, while some Muslim and Christian traditions hold that it wasn't fig leaves that Adam and Eve were wearing in the Garden of Eden but banana leaves; not an apple that they ate, but a banana.

EGGS

The egg – whether chicken egg or caviar – is an ancient symbol of fertility all over the world. That renowned lover, Catherine the Great, was convinced of caviar's potency when, urged to produce an heir to the throne, she declared, 'Bring me some caviar, and tonight at supper, send me the best built of my officers.'

FIGS

Throughout history, figs have been associated with love and fertility. Adam and Eve wore fig leaves, Cleopatra lived almost solely on figs, and a man opening a fig and eating it in front of his lover is believed to be a powerfully erotic act. An open fig is said to be reminiscent of the female genitalia, which is what gives this fruit its sexy edge.

HONEY

Apart from its widely known medicinal properties, honey was hailed as a potent aphrodisiac as far back as 500 BC. In some traditions, honey was drunk at weddings, and the term 'honeymoon' refers to the time when bride and groom went off into seclusion to drink a honey concoction until the first new moon after their wedding.

Poultry Matters

CHOOSING POULTRY

Whatever poultry you are looking for and whether it's fresh or frozen, look for plump-breasted birds with blemish-free skin (its breed and the food it's been reared on will dictate the colour of the skin, but it should be even-coloured, with no patchy spots). A fresh bird should look moist, not wet. For fuller flavour, go for free-range birds.

STORING POULTRY

* Eat your fresh poultry within two days of buying it, storing it in the fridge.

* If the bird is frozen, make sure you get it home and into the freezer as quickly as possible after purchase, and use it by the date shown on the label.

* Any uncooked fresh poultry should be taken out of the packaging it came in, placed on a plate and covered loosely with foil, then stored on the bottom shelf of the fridge to stop any juices from falling onto other food.

* If your bird comes with giblets intact, take them out of the bird and store in a separate bowl in the fridge.

* Before cooking chicken or turkey, rinse the cavity out well and pat dry with kitchen paper.

✱ Cooked chicken can be kept in the fridge for two to three days.

What shall I do with the giblets?
The bird's neck, heart, liver and gizzard are usually found in a plastic bag within the bird when you buy it (although it's rare to see giblets in ready-prepared supermarket birds anymore). Traditionally chopped and used as an ingredient in the stuffing, giblets are also used for making stock for soup and gravy.

JOINTING AN UNCOOKED BIRD

Jointing your poultry will give you eight equal portions – two wings, two drumsticks, two breasts and two thighs. First, take off the drumsticks and thighs and cut through the joint that connects them. Then, holding the wing, take a sharp knife or a pair of poultry shears and make a deep incision down the centre of the breast, right through to the bone. Keeping as close to the bone as possible, slice the flesh away from the breastbone, cutting it free from the wing where it's joined to the carcass, and repeat on the other side. Finally, cut the wings free from the carcass.

WHAT'S THE GAME?

Game birds include grouse, guinea fowl, partridge, pheasant and quail, and they are often chosen for special occasions. But choosing which to buy shouldn't be too hard if you know what your recipe requires. All game birds are low in fat, and have to be cooked carefully because they can become dry and tough if cooked too long. The rule of thumb is to select young, tender birds for quick cooking, grilling, stir-frying and roasting, and older birds for slower methods like stewing, since the moisture in the stew will help tenderize the flesh and draw out that gamey flavour. Ask your butcher for further advice.

HANGING GAME BIRDS

When a game bird is hung, the enzymes in the flesh undergo a chemical reaction, which tenderizes the meat. The longer the bird is hung, the richer and more 'gamey' the flavour. By the time you buy it your game bird should have been hung already, but if you are given game that hasn't been pre-hung, make sure you put it in a cold, dark, well-ventilated room such as a garage or shed and that the bird or birds are hung clear of any surface and do not touch each other. Most game birds are hung for up to ten days.

Poultry Sense

ROASTING A WHOLE BIRD

Poultry and game birds benefit from having a little fat added when roasting to keep the flesh moist as it cooks. One method to help keep the bird moist is to insert half an onion into the cavity before roasting. Otherwise, you can put a few small pats of butter on the skin or add streaky bacon.

TESTING A BIRD FOR DONENESS

After roasting your bird for the recommended time, always check it is properly cooked by piercing the flesh with a fork and pressing down so you can see the juices bubble through the skin. If the juices run clear and there's no sign of blood, the bird is cooked.

MAKING GRAVY

Remove the bird from the tin and pour off all but about a tablespoon of fat. Put the tin on a low heat and sprinkle in a tablespoon of plain flour, stirring well. Gradually whisk in 500 ml (approx 18 fl oz) of stock or water. Increase the heat and bring the gravy to a boil. Simmer, still whisking, for a couple of minutes, check the seasoning and serve.

ON THE BARBIE

There's nothing like a chicken drumstick cooked over coals. The heat crisps the skin and the flavour is intense.

MARINADES

Try giving your drumsticks extra flavour by marinating them for at least an hour in the fridge before barbecuing.

* For a Mediterranean flavour, mix olive oil, crushed garlic and chopped fresh herbs.

* For a spicy aromatic flavour, try mixing crushed chillies, crushed garlic, chopped fresh rosemary and olive oil.

* For a hint of India, mix plain yoghurt with a teaspoon of Indian curry paste and chopped fresh coriander.

TIPS ON COOKING GAME BIRDS

* Add lard or slices of streaky bacon to the breasts of young birds, both to keep them moist and to add flavour.

* Young birds are better for roasting than older ones, which work well braised or casseroled.

* Marinating a bird before cooking will help tenderize the flesh as well as flavouring and moistening it.

Chicken with lemon thyme

This is a fantastic and fragrant way to cook chicken in a chicken brick – a clay pot that encloses the meat, resulting in tender, moist and flavoursome meals.

You will need:

> *garlic clove*
> *a whole chicken*
> *Dijon mustard*
> *freshly ground sea salt*
> *freshly ground black pepper*
> *handful fresh chervil*
> *handful fresh tarragon*
> *handful fresh lemon thyme*
> *handful fresh parsley*
> *handful fresh marjoram*
> *handful fresh dill*
> *1 tablespoon extra virgin olive oil*

Rub a crushed garlic clove on the inside of the chicken brick. Take your chicken and paint it with the Dijon mustard, sprinkle with sea salt and black pepper and place in the brick. Add a handful each of the chopped herbs, drizzle with a tablespoon of extra virgin olive oil and put the lid on the brick. Follow the recommended cooking time for your chicken. About 15 minutes before the end of the cooking time, take the lid off the chicken brick and let it brown in the oven.

Perfect Carving

You have your roast joint or bird – cooked to perfection, looking succulent and delicious – but you know in your heart of hearts that the moment you start to carve, your lack of precision with the knife will ruin your efforts and the roast will look like a disaster on a plate. There are secrets to carving several different roasts, but a few principles that apply to all:

* Your carving knife blade should be long enough to cut the breast of a large bird or large roast into neat slices, so should extend about 5 cm beyond the meat on both sides to accommodate the sawing action.

* Letting the roast or bird rest for 10 to 15 minutes after cooking results in firmer, juicier meat that's easier to carve.

* Always carve across the grain of the meat, not parallel to its fibres.

* Make sure your serving platter is warm.

CHICKEN OR TURKEY

* Cut each leg from the body. Separate the thigh from the drumstick and place on a warm plate.

* Make a deep horizontal cut just above the wing and through the breast until the knife touches the breastbone.

✳ Make a series of vertical cuts through the breast meat, pressing the knife all the way down to the first horizontal cut.

> *Poultry is for cookery what canvas is for painting, and the cap of Fortunatus for the charlatans. It is served to us boiled, roasted, hot or cold, whole or in portions, with or without sauce, and always with equal success.*
>
> **JEAN-ANTHELME BRILLAT-SAVARIN**

DUCK

✳ Remove each wing by cutting through the joint between the wing and the body.

✳ Remove each leg by cutting through the skin around the leg, then slice down between the thigh and body to reveal the joint and cut through the joint to separate.

✳ Hold the knife blade at about a 45-degree angle to the duck and cut long, thin slices from one side of the breast. Repeat on the other side.

RIB ROAST

* Ask your butcher to remove the chine bone so that you can carve the roast between the rib bones.

* Place the roast rib-side down on a cutting board. Holding the knife about 5 mm in from the edge, slice towards the ribs.

* Cut along the edge of the rib bone to release the slice.

* As each rib bone is exposed, cut it.

LAMB - RACK

* Place the rack rib-side down on a cutting board and, holding it steady, use a sawing action to cut between the ribs.

LAMB - LEG

* Cut a slice from the thin side of the leg and turn the leg cut-side down.

* Make a vertical cut to the bone about 2 to 3 cm from the shank.

* From the shank end, make a horizontal cut, parallel to the bone, releasing the slice of meat.

* Continue with even slices, cutting perpendicular to the bone and working away from the shank.

* Turn the leg over and cut long slices following the line of the bone.

A WHOLE HAM

* Place the ham on a cutting board and, using a two-pronged fork, cut a few slices from the thin side of the ham so that it will lie flat.

* Turn the ham over onto the cut surface and remove a small wedge of meat at the shank end. Cut even slices along the ham right to the bone.

* Work the blade under the slices to release them from the bone.

Et voilà! Your roasts will always do you proud.

Roasting Times

You have the perfect joint, game or bird, and it's ready to go in the oven. But how do you know how long to cook it for?
There are a few general tips to ensure that your roast is perfect. Firstly make sure all food is piping hot and fully cooked before serving. Make sure all frozen items are fully defrosted before cooking. Cook stuffing separately to make sure it is cooked through. To test poultry for 'doneness' pierce with a fork and make sure the bird's juices run clear and with no sign of blood. When done, remove the meat from the oven and leave it to stand or 'rest' for 10 to 20 minutes before serving.

Meat		Time
Beef	*rare*	20 mins per 450 g (1 lb) plus 20 mins
	medium	25 mins per 450 g (1 lb) plus 25 mins
	well done	30 mins per 450 g (1 lb) plus 30 mins
Lamb	*rare*	20 mins per 450 g (1 lb) plus 20 mins
	medium	25 mins per 450 g (1 lb) plus 25 mins
	well done	30 mins per 450 g (1 lb) plus 30 mins
Pork		35 mins per 450 g (1 lb) plus 35 mins
Chicken		20 mins per 450 g (1 lb) plus 20 mins
Turkey		25 mins per 450 g (1 lb) plus 25 mins
Pheasant		25 mins per 450 g (1 lb)
Venison		25 mins per 450 g (1 lb)
Hare		20 mins per 450 g (1 lb)

Cooking with Chillies

The huge variety of chillies now available makes it difficult to choose the right type for your taste: some can literally blow your head off; others could be disappointingly mild for some palates. Chillies get their heat from the presence of the volatile oil capsaicin, and the amount of this oil present in each chilli is measured on the Scoville scale, first developed by Wilbur L Scoville in 1912. A sweet pepper that contains no capsaicin at all has a Scoville rating of zero, while some of the hottest chillies such as the eye-watering habanero or scotch bonnet have a rating of 300,000 on the Scoville scale.

HOT, HOTTER, HOTTEST

The milder chillies can vary in the amount of heat they give off, so the following list is only a rough guide from the hottest down to the mildest.

* Habanero – Mexican and Caribbean dishes that need intense heat – use with care.

* Scotch bonnet – Mexican and Caribbean dishes that need intense heat – use with care.

* Bird's eye – Mexican dishes – use sparingly.

* Hot gold spike – Mexican dishes – use sparingly.

* Thai – Thai sauces, curries and rice dishes – use sparingly.

* Ethiopian – sauces, curries and rice dishes – use sparingly.

* Yellow wax – Thai dishes or curries – varies from mild to very hot, so use with care.

* Jalapeno – chutneys, pickles and salsas – 2 to 3 per dish or according to taste.

* Serrano – Mexican, Caribbean or Thai dishes – 2 to 3 per dish or according to taste.

* Anaheim – any recipe where a moderate amount of heat is required – 2 to 3 per dish or according to taste.

COOK'S TIP

Capsaicin is most concentrated in the chilli's seeds and pith, which is why, when preparing hot chillies, you should always wear rubber gloves or use a knife, and, above all, avoid rubbing your eyes.

* Poblano – used in Spanish tapas, can be roasted or grilled – use whole or chopped.

* Cascabel – roast or grill, use in salsas – use whole or chopped.

* Pimento – use as recipe requires – use whole or chopped.

TABASCO SAUCE

Hot and peppery, Tabasco will spice up any dish that's turned out rather more bland than you'd hoped. But don't splash it about too much; used with care it is a very useful store cupboard staple.

CHILLI POWDER, CAYENNE PEPPER AND CHILLI FLAKES

While chilli powder is made from a variety of chillies that range from mild to eye-wateringly hot, cayenne pepper is ground from a particular variety originally from the Cayenne region of French Guiana. Said to have significant health benefits, cayenne is fiery and has a distinctive flavour. Chilli flakes are crushed, flaked chillies and add immediate flavour to the dish – perfect on pizzas and in casseroles instead of whole chillies.

Eight Cooks Who Changed Our Kitchens

JEAN ANTHELME BRILLAT-SAVARIN (1755-1826)

French politician and lawyer, Brillat-Savarin's seminal work, *The Physiology of Taste: or, Meditations on Transcendental Gastronomy*, was published in 1825, shortly before his death. He is hailed as the first gastronome to treat the 'art' of cookery as a science, and his book, which was published anonymously, began to alter peoples' perception of food and nutrition.

MRS BEETON (1836-65)

Isabella Mary Beeton is the most famous cookery writer in British history. Published when she was only twenty-five, her most famous work, *Mrs Beeton's Book of Household Management*, was a definitive guide on how to run a Victorian household and also contained over 900 recipes. Mrs Beeton changed the way in which recipes were set out on the page, putting the ingredients list at the beginning of the recipe rather than within the recipe itself. Unfortunately, she did not live to see the success of her work, dying at the age of twenty-eight.

AUGUSTE ESCOFFIER (1846-1935)

George Auguste Escoffier was a master chef, restaurateur and writer who revolutionized the way in which restaurants were organized. At the age of nineteen he was made sous-chef at one of Paris's finest restaurants, Le Petit Moulin Rouge, and three years later he was made head chef. He formed a partnership with César Ritz, and the two men worked together at the Savoy in London and went on to establish a number of famous hotels around the world, and cement Escoffier's growing reputation as one of the world's finest chefs. Escoffier's major work, *Le Guide Culinaire*, published in 1903, contains over 5,000 recipes and is used even today as a textbook for classic French cooking.

FANNY CRADOCK (1909-94)

Fanny Cradock made her debut on British television in 1955 and, by the late 1950s, along with her partner Johnnie Cradock (she didn't actually marry Johnnie until the mid-1970s), she brought the cost-effective 'glamour' of French cuisine into Britain's kitchens. Her booklets, published to tie in with the recipes demonstrated on the show, were instantly successful, and she has been hailed as the saviour of post-war British cooking.

JULIA CHILD (1912-2004)

An American cook, author and television presenter, Julia Child's most famous book, published in 1961, was *Mastering the Art of French Cooking*. Written with two other graduates from the

Cordon Bleu cookery school, the book was hailed by the *New York Times* as 'the finest volume on French cooking ever published in English'. After the book's success, Child was offered a television series, *The French Chef*, and went on to become America's first celebrity chef.

ELIZABETH DAVID (1913-92)

Elizabeth David's lasting legacy was to bring real Mediterranean cooking into British households. Author of over a dozen classic books, including *Mediterranean Food*, *French Provincial Cooking* and *An Omelette and a Glass of Wine*, David is credited with bringing ingredients such as garlic, olive oil and pasta into our kitchens.

MARGUERITE PATTEN (1915-)

Author of over 170 books (which are reputed to have sold over seventeen million copies worldwide) Marguerite Patten was one of the first celebrity chefs to appear on British television. Her inventive and engaging presentation style has made her the doyenne of British cookery writing and a much-loved figure, still writing and broadcasting today.

JOEL ROBUCHON (1945-)

French chef and restaurateur Joel Robuchon's extraordinary skill, style and attention to detail have won him many plaudits, including seventeen coveted Michelin stars. He began his career at the age of fifteen in his native Poitiers, and opened his first restaurant, Jamin, in Paris in 1981. By 1990, the influential French restaurant guide *Gault Millau* voted Joel Robouchon 'Chef of the Century'. Closing his restaurant in 1996 to pursue other interests, he returned to the business in 2003, opening fourteen restaurants around the world.

Cooks are in some ways very much like actors; they must be fit and strong, since acting and cooking are two of the most exacting professions. They must be blessed – or cursed, whichever way you care to look at it – with what is called the artistic temperament, which means that if they are to act or cook at all well, it cannot be for duds or dummies.

ANDRÉ SIMON
The Concise Encyclopaedia of Gastronomy (1952)

In a Stew

The best stews and casseroles are usually the simplest and least complicated to make. What they rely on is the quality and freshness of the ingredients you use, rather than the additional flavourings and other items you cook with the meat, so make sure when cooking these simple stews that you use the best available cuts.

Beef stew

Known in my home as 'second-day stew', this recipe calls for a cooking time of three hours, but we think it's actually better left overnight and heated thoroughly the next day.

You will need:

1 large onion
3 tablespoons oil
1 large red pepper, de-seeded and thinly sliced
450g (1lb) braising steak, trimmed
and cut into chunks
225g (8oz) ripe tomatoes, peeled and halved
300ml (10 floz) beef stock
1 bouquet garni
freshly ground sea salt
freshly ground black pepper
1 tablespoon fresh parsley, chopped

Fry the onion in the oil until it is just browning. Add the peppers and the meat and cook, stirring frequently, until the meat is well browned. Pre-heat the oven to 160°C/325°F. Add the tomatoes, stock and bouquet garni and bring to a boil. Cover and cook in the oven for 2½–3 hours. Season well, remove the bouquet garni and sprinkle with parsley before serving.

Peppered fish stew

I love fish stew and this doesn't overwhelm the main ingredient. Though the peppercorns are piquant, they don't dominate the dish.
You will need:

2 small onions, cut into rings
55g (2oz) butter
225g (8oz) French beans, trimmed and halved
280g (10oz) can sweetcorn
150ml (5 floz) fish stock or milk
450g (1lb) cod or monkfish
4 tablespoons double cream
1 teaspoon fresh green peppercorns
sea salt
sprig fresh dill

Fry the onions gently in the butter. Add the beans, corn and stock and bring to a boil. Simmer for about 10 minutes. Meanwhile, skin the fish and cut into large chunks. Add to the pan, along with the cream and peppercorns. Cook gently for about 10 minutes. Season to taste and add a little fresh dill to serve.

Chicken paprika casserole

You will need:

> *1.5 kg (3 lb 5 oz) chicken, jointed (see page 27)*
> *125 ml (4 fl oz) chicken stock (approx)*
> *125 ml (4 fl oz) dry white wine (approx)*
> *50 g (1¾ oz) butter*
> *sprig fresh tarragon*
> *1 onion, chopped*
> *20 g (¾ oz) flour*
> *1 tablespoon paprika*
> *450 g (1 lb) tomatoes, peeled and quartered*
> *1 clove garlic, crushed*
> *1 bay leaf*
> *freshly ground sea salt*
> *freshly ground black pepper*
> *75 ml (2½ fl oz) single cream*

Pre-heat the oven to 190°C/375°F. Place the chicken joints in an ovenproof casserole dish with the stock and the wine. Dot with half the butter, add the tarragon, cover with a lid and cook in the oven for 30 minutes. Drain the chicken juices into a bowl and keep the chicken joints hot. Fry the onion in the remaining butter, add the paprika and flour, and then gradually stir in the reserved chicken juices. Add the tomatoes, garlic, bay leaf and seasoning. Bring to a boil and add a little more stock if the consistency is too thick. Pour the sauce over the chicken joints and return to the oven for a further 30 minutes. Remove the bay leaf and stir in the cream just before serving.

Chicken Provençal

Hearty and warming, this is fantastic with saffron-infused rice.
You will need:

> *1.5 kg (3 lb 5 oz) chicken, jointed*
> *sunflower oil for frying*
> *2 onions, chopped*
> *2 cloves garlic, crushed*
> *2 green peppers, de-seeded and diced*
> *125 ml (4 fl oz) dry white wine*
> *6 tomatoes, skinned and chopped*
> *1 tablespoon tomato purée*
> *1 bay leaf*
> *1 teaspoon dried oregano (2 teaspoons fresh)*
> *freshly ground sea salt*
> *freshly ground black pepper*

Heat the oil in a large, flameproof casserole and fry the chicken,
onions, garlic and green peppers until the chicken is browned.
Add the wine, tomatoes, tomato purée, bay leaf and oregano.
Season well, cover and simmer for 1–1¼ hours. Remove the bay
leaf, adjust the seasoning and serve.

> *I cook with wine.*
> *Sometimes I even add it to the food.*
> **W. C. FIELDS**

Five Oils to Try

There are many different general and speciality oils available now, but only a few that you need to know about to get the best from your cooking.

EXTRA VIRGIN OLIVE OIL

This oil is obtained by pressing olives when they come off the tree – without any other process or treatment. If it just says 'Olive oil' on the bottle, you know that the oil has been refined in some way. The price difference between olive oil and extra virgin olive oil can be vast, so use olive oil for frying and roasting and save the extra virgin for dressings.

SUNFLOWER OIL

Ideal for use as a general cooking oil and, because of its very mild taste, at those times when you don't want a strong intrusive flavour, such as in making mayonnaise, baking and frying.

SESAME OIL

This is a very flavoursome oil that should be used sparingly as a drizzling and dressing oil for salads and in stir-fries rather than in general cooking.

WALNUT OIL

With a delicate, nutty flavour, this one is perfect in a salad dressing, drizzled over steamed vegetables or for use in baking.

AVOCADO OIL

Made from pressing the flesh of avocados, this oil is a fantastic complement to seafood and salads, and drizzled over roast chicken.

> *It takes four men to dress a salad: a wise man for the salt, a madman for the pepper, a miser for the vinegar, and a spendthrift for the oil.*
>
> **ANONYMOUS**

In the Raw

Cooking enhances the taste of many foods – some are virtually inedible unless cooked – but the downside of cooking can be a loss of important vitamins and other nutrients. So raw foods should have a special place in any healthy diet. We may actually eat more raw foods than we think: milk, cheese, fruit, salads, nuts, and many types of cured and salted meat and fish are all raw or nearly raw products. Health concerns may have discouraged us from eating raw beef, for example, but on the whole, as long as raw food is prepared with scrupulous attention to hygiene there is normally little or no health risk in eating it. However for most of us the reality is that, apart from the occasional Japanese meal of sushi or sashimi, most of our raw food comes from fruit and vegetables – so here are a few tips on how to make the most of them.

HOW TO PRESERVE THE NUTRIENTS IN YOUR FRUIT AND VEGETABLES

✱ Avoid peeling fruit and vegetables, as many of the essential nutrients and fibre are found just under the skin. Instead, just wash your fruit, and scrub vegetable skin with a vegetable brush under running water.

* Don't buy processed vegetables in the supermarket. The prepared vegetables and salads you see on the shelves will have been washed, peeled and bagged some time previously and contain little or no vitamins and minerals, which will have been lost in the processing.

* Many fruits and vegetables respond well to freezing, especially when they are frozen immediately after harvesting. Frozen peas, Brussels sprouts and spinach, and berry fruits such as raspberries and blueberries are particularly good from the freezer as they retain most of their vitamin and mineral content.

* Fruits and vegetables that don't freeze well include lettuce, tomatoes, celery, potatoes, garlic and onions.

* Buy your fruit and vegetables as and when you need them, don't let them sit in the fridge for too long. Buy them from a reliable source so that you know they are fresh.

* Wash your veggies just before eating to prevent any further vitamin loss. The longer vegetables stand in water, the more vitamins and minerals leach out to be lost forever.

* When preparing vegetables such as cauliflower or broccoli, think before discarding too much of the stalk as these are rich in vitamins.

* Don't cut fruit and vegetables into small pieces as this exposes more of the surface to the air and nutrients are lost.

Vegetables

A general rule of thumb when choosing all vegetables is to try to go for locally grown produce as it should be tastier and much fresher than anything that has had to travel from far-flung places. Go to a local farm shop or farmers' market, greengrocer or supermarket where the turn over of stock will be fast.

Many vegetables are sensitive to a chemical called ethylene, which is emitted by some fruits and vegetables.

* Apples, bananas, pears, peaches, plums and melons, mushrooms and tomatoes emit ethylene.

* Aubergines, leafy greens, beans, carrots, cucumbers, peas, peppers and potatoes absorb ethylene

Ethylene can help in the ripening process, but it can also lead to your lettuce turning brown, your carrots going limp and your tomatoes losing their flavour. The trick is to keep the two types away from each other while storing.

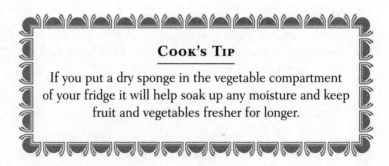

COOK'S TIP

If you put a dry sponge in the vegetable compartment of your fridge it will help soak up any moisture and keep fruit and vegetables fresher for longer.

TYPICAL STEAMING TIMES

Steaming is much the best way to cook vegetables. Avoid that soggy mess that boiled vegetables can become, and be healthier into the bargain!

* Asparagus spears – 5 to 10 minutes

* Broccoli – 8 minutes

* Brussels sprouts – 10 minutes

* Cabbage – 10 minutes

* Carrots – 10 minutes

* Cauliflower – 8 minutes

* Fennel – 10 minutes

* Green beans – 8 minutes

* Peas – 3 minutes

* Potatoes (new) – 12 minutes

* Spinach – 1 to 2 minutes

COOK'S TIP

Try not to keep your vegetables in plastic bags. Many vegetables will stay fresher for longer in paper bags. If you do store them in plastic bags, make sure they are perforated so that air can circulate.

If you do boil your vegetables, make sure you keep the water and use it in other dishes (such as stews and soups). It makes the perfect base for stock and is full of the minerals and vitamins that have leached from the vegetables you boiled.

> *Life expectancy would grow by leaps and bounds*
> *if green vegetables smelled as good as bacon.*
> **DOUG LARSON**

ONIONS, GARLIC AND LEEKS

What would we do without vegetables from this family? I cook with onions and garlic almost every day, in one way or another, they add flavour to stews, pilaffs, pasta, curries, salads – the lot! Additionally, garlic has many health benefits, and leeks contain useful amounts of vitamin C, calcium and iron. From yellow onions through red onions to shallots and pickling onions, they all have a fantastic flavour to impart. When choosing onions look for a good, bright colour and no blemishes, soft spots or signs of sprouting. Onions that have been exposed to frost may feel soft, so look out for this in the winter months. Garlic bulbs

should look plump, and the skin should be clear – take care to avoid garlic with any signs of sprouting. Look for leeks with bright green tops and milky white heads.

* Store onions in a cool, dry place, where they will keep well for about 4 weeks. Do not keep in the fridge as they will go soft.

* Garlic should be stored in a cool dark place. The bulbs will begin to sprout if the air is too damp.

* Leeks can be stored in the fridge or in a cool dark place, where they will keep for up to a week.

COOK'S TIPS

* To get rid of the smell of onions and garlic from your fingers, rub your hands with a piece of fresh ginger.

* To peel fiddly garlic bulbs, drop them into boiling water for a minute; the skin will be loosened and come off very easily.

* Prevent tears when chopping onions by leaving the root end intact while chopping.

* The best way to get all the mud and grit out of leeks is first to trim off any ragged ends at the top, then cut the vegetable from its green top down to the beginnings of its white head, so you can fan the leaves out and rinse with cold water.

CELERY, FENNEL AND ASPARAGUS

There's nothing like the bite of crisp celery, the taste of sweet fennel or the melting charms of perfectly prepared asparagus. These are the most revered vegetables, with both fennel and asparagus appearing among the celebrated list of aphrodisiac foods! When choosing celery, the stalks should be tightly packed and blemish-free, with fresh-looking leaves on top. Fennel bulbs should be crisp and creamy white, compact and free of discolouration, with fresh green leaves. Asparagus stalks (which come in three types: green, white and purple) should be brightly coloured, firm and straight, the buds should be tight. Try to avoid spears with tough, woody stems.

All three should be eaten while they are fresh. Fennel in particular can lose its unique flavour if stored for too long.

* Store celery in the fridge for up to 2 weeks (and see Cook's Tip, below).

* Asparagus is best stored by trimming the ends off and standing in a glass with a little water in the bottom; cover loosely with a perforated plastic bag and place in the fridge for up to 2 days.

* Fennel can be stored in the fridge for 2 to 3 days.

COOK'S TIP

Revive your limp celery by standing it in a jar of water.

Store Cupboard Staples

There are certain 'essentials' that you'll always find useful in your cooking. Ingredients like pasta, rice and noodles are the basis of tasty and easy-to-cook meals. Of course, stocking your store cupboard is a matter of your taste, but here are some pointers as to which items will come in very useful if you have them to hand.

OILS

Olive oil – extra virgin olive oil is best for quality and flavour and is a great staple for salad dressings and marinades.
Vegetable oil – sunflower oil is good for frying.

SAUCES AND CONDIMENTS

Mustards – wholegrain, English and Dijon
Soy sauce
Sea salt
Whole black peppercorns
Vinegars, malt and balsamic
Tabasco sauce
Tomato ketchup
Tomato purée
Yeast extract
Worcestershire sauce

FOR THE FRIDGE

Try not to over-buy on fresh produce, it can be a waste of food and money, and you shouldn't store items like meat and fish for long anyway – it's much better to buy them fresh when you know you're going to eat them. If you're working and do your shopping in one fell swoop at the weekend, depending on your tastes, try to plan so that you have two meat- or poultry-based meals, one fish-based meal and two vegetable-based meals during the week, so that you have variety and flexibility in your diet. Things you can keep stocked in your fridge are:

Butter
Cheese
Eggs
Milk
Mayonnaise

FOR THE VEGETABLE RACK

Onions
Garlic
Potatoes
Lemons and Limes

DRIED GOODS

Rice – long-grain, Indian, risotto
Pasta – spaghetti, penne, lasagne
Noodles – Chinese egg noodles

Dried herbs and spices – oregano, sage, rosemary, marjoram and dried mixed herbs; curry powder, dried chillies, turmeric, coriander seeds, cumin seeds, fennel seeds and a mixed spice should be sufficient for basic recipes.

Cans – chopped tomatoes, canned tuna, anchovies in brine, red kidney beans

Stock – beef or lamb, and chicken and fish stock cubes, plus a jar of vegetable bouillon

Flour – self-raising and plain

MISCELLANEOUS

Olives
Chocolate
Tea and coffee
Sugar – granulated, caster, soft brown
and Demerara sugars, plus clear honey

Perfect Pasta

The secret to real Italian pasta is that it should not be drenched in sauce. The pasta itself should be the main part of the dish, with the sauce acting as an accompaniment to the pasta. The fact is that most of us (me included) actually add too much to a pasta sauce and take away from the depth of the dish by overcomplicating things. The best idea when making sauce is to use a little of the best quality item, rather than a lot of something that's poorer quality. For example, use good, fresh garlic or really ripe and fresh tomatoes; go for a handful of fresh herbs rather than a sprinkling of dried. Make your own pesto sauce with a handful of basil, some pine nuts, a clove of garlic, some extra virgin olive oil, and grated Pecorino cheese, all crushed together with a mortar and pestle.

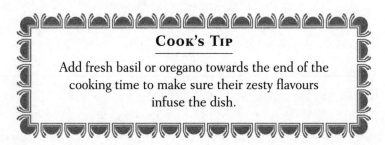

Cook's Tip

Add fresh basil or oregano towards the end of the
cooking time to make sure their zesty flavours
infuse the dish.

WHICH PASTA WORKS BEST WITH WHICH SAUCE?

An Italian cook will always ask what sorts of pasta are available before deciding which sauce to make. Penne and fusilli, for example, are best with creamy, thick sauces, whereas finer pastas such as spaghetti or linguine work better with thinner, oil-based sauces that will thoroughly coat the pasta. Sheets of pasta, such as lasagne, are good with meaty sauces.

COOKING TIMES

You should calculate the pasta's cooking time from the moment the water has come back to a boil after the pasta has been submerged. Always test the pasta before draining.

* Fresh pasta – 1 to 3 minutes

* Fresh stuffed pasta – 3 to 7 minutes

* Dried long pasta – 8 to 15 minutes

* Dried pasta shapes – 10 to 12 minutes

Testing pasta for doneness
The Italian way is to cook pasta until it is *al dente* – firm to bite, not mushy. Towards the end of the recommended cooking time, take a piece of pasta from the pot and bite into it. It should be tender without any hint of rawness, but with just a little resistance to the bite. If it is done, drain the pasta immediately, otherwise return to the heat and test again after 30 to 60 seconds.

DIFFERENT PASTA SHAPES AVAILABLE

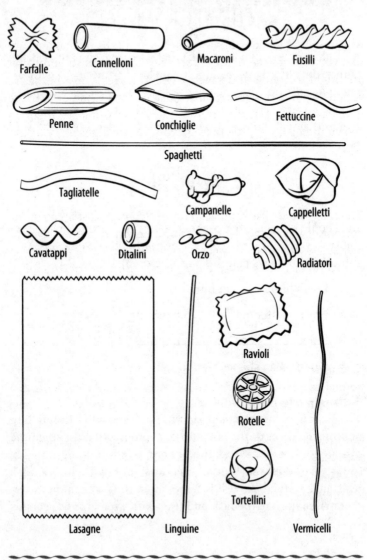

Farfalle

Cannelloni

Macaroni

Fusilli

Penne

Conchiglie

Fettuccine

Spaghetti

Tagliatelle

Campanelle

Cappelletti

Cavatappi

Ditalini

Orzo

Radiatori

Ravioli

Rotelle

Tortellini

Lasagne

Linguine

Vermicelli

Cooking with Herbs

Maximize the wonderful flavours of your herbs by making sure that you prepare them just before use. Choose fresh herbs that are bright in colour and have no wilted leaves. Most herbs are very delicate and will only last a day or two. Chop or tear the herbs as you need them because the longer you leave them on the chopping board, the more flavour they will lose.

STORING

Most herbs are best kept fresh by storing in a plastic bag in the bottom of the fridge. Coriander and rosemary are best stored by placing the stems in a glass of cold water, while parsley can either be kept in the fridge or sprinkled with water and wrapped in paper towels.

PREPARING AND USING FRESH HERBS

Stripping the leaves
Some herbs, such as chervil and coriander, have soft stems that can be chopped and cooked along with the leaves, but most stems are tough and woody and the leaves need to be stripped from the stems before cooking. To strip tough stems, hold the bottom of the stem firmly in one hand and use the thumb and forefinger of the other hand on either side of the stem to pinch the leaves off as you drag the stem towards you.

With tender stems such as dill and fennel, strip the leaves from the bottom of the stem, pulling the leaf sprays away from the main stem and stripping out any tough stems from the sprays as you work.

Making a paste
Herbs can be pounded into a paste using a mortar and pestle. You could use a food processor, but if you only want herbs for one dish, a mortar and pestle is much less hard work on the washing up.

Chopping leaves
The flavour of herbs is found in the essential oils they contain, but the more surface area exposed in chopping, the more essential oils are lost. So, if you chop herbs very finely, you may discover that they lose a great deal of their flavour in cooking, whereas if you roughly chop your herbs you will find that they keep their flavour for longer in the cooking process.

A large, sharp knife is all you need for chopping herbs, but some cooks swear by a mezzaluna, a curved two-handled chopper that slices with a rocking motion, backwards and forwards.

If you use a large knife, the best method of chopping herbs is to lay the herbs on your chopping board and, with one hand

holding the point of the blade on the surface of the board over the herbs, use the other hand to chop up and down in a rocking motion, back and forth over the herbs. When you have gone from one side of the herbs to the other, pile them together again and repeat as necessary until they are chopped as finely as you need them.

DRYING HERBS

Not all herbs respond well to drying. Those with tough, woody stems, such as oregano and thyme, dry well and retain their flavour. Those with softer stems, such as basil and parsley, lose their flavour almost completely (but remember, you can freeze the softer herb, see page 66). For the best flavour, dry herbs just before their flower buds open, when their essential oils are at their highest concentration.

When preparing herbs for drying, make sure you discard any discoloured leaves. Tie the herbs together in small bunches and hang in a well-ventilated, cool place, out of direct sunlight. You will know the herbs are dry when the leaves feel brittle. Strip the leaves from the stems and store in an airtight container.

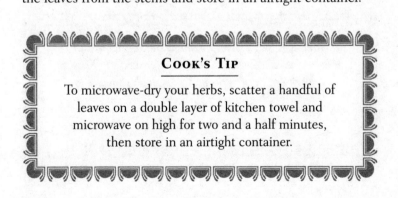

COOK'S TIP

To microwave-dry your herbs, scatter a handful of leaves on a double layer of kitchen towel and microwave on high for two and a half minutes, then store in an airtight container.

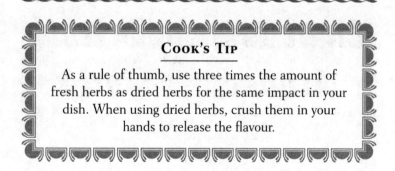

COOK'S TIP

As a rule of thumb, use three times the amount of fresh herbs as dried herbs for the same impact in your dish. When using dried herbs, crush them in your hands to release the flavour.

FREEZING HERBS

Softer herbs such as basil and parsley do not respond well to the drying process, so you can chop them and freeze them instead. Wash and dry the herbs well, discarding any discoloured or old stems, chop them as required and freeze in small pots or freezer ice-cube trays. When they have frozen, pop the herbs into plastic bags for storage. They will keep their flavour for about three or four months. When you need them, just add a cube to your dish for instant flavour. Fantastic if you grow your own herbs.

Tomatoes and oregano make it Italian; wine and tarragon make it French. Sour cream makes it Russian; lemon and cinnamon make it Greek. Soy sauce makes it Chinese; garlic makes it good.

ALICE MAY BROCK (of *Alice's Restaurant*)

Eight Foul Foods from Around the World

KOPI LUWAK COFFEE

The plump red berries from a normal coffee tree in the Sumatran jungle are a delicacy for the luwak, a type of civet native to south-east Asia. The luwak eats the berries and when they are digested, yes, they are passed in the usual way. Once picked from luwak droppings on the jungle floor, the beans are scrubbed clean and ground. Once brewed, Kopi Luwak is said to have a nutty, quite bitter flavour, but is hailed as not only the priciest but also the best coffee in the world. I was unable to find out who first decided to rummage through the animal droppings in order to try the coffee.

BIRDS' NEST SOUP

It is the saliva from the male swiftlet that creates the highly prized nest for Bird's Nest Soup. They carry a high price due to the length of time it takes for the bird to create the nest, and the increasing difficulty collectors are having in gathering their crop. The soup can be savoury or sweet. The savoury soup is usually made with chicken stock, quails eggs and mushrooms; the sweet soup is simply water, sugar and nest. The nests themselves are tasteless and glutinous, but they are highly sought after for their purported medicinal and aphrodisiacal qualities. Harvesting of nests has sharply depleted the swiftlet populations in some locations.

CASU FRAZIGU CHEESE

Although the Italian government has banned its sale, this cheese is still lauded as a true Italian delicacy. Casu Frazigu is basically Pecorino cheese that is left to ferment – or decompose – after the introduction of the fly *Piophila casei*. The fly deposits its eggs on the aging cheese, the maggots hatch and they move through the cheese excreting enzymes that make it very soft, and *very* smelly. Apparently the maggots can leap up to 15 cm, enabling the cheese buyer to hear their cheese rather than just smell or taste it. Some aficionados scrape the maggots from the cheese before eating it; others do not.

SNAKE WINE

A Vietnamese delicacy in which the restaurateur makes a slit along the snake's belly and drains its blood into a vat of rice wine. Enjoyed in shots, this is followed by a meal of snake meat. Most people agree the drink is highly unpleasant, but locals believe it has healing and aphrodisiacal qualities.

FUGU

The Japanese word for pufferfish or blowfish, Fugu contains lethal levels of the poison tetrodotoxin, and only licensed, trained chefs are allowed to prepare it. Commonly served very thinly sliced as sashimi, Fugu is also eaten in cooked dishes. Although deemed pretty tasteless by most people, the fish is prized for its texture and for the prickling sensation caused by the small levels of poison in the meat. Apparently, because of the strict regulations on preparation, the number of deaths due to Fugu consumption is decreasing.

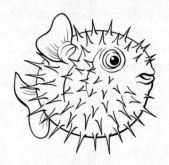

FERTILIZED DUCK EGG (BALUT)

A highly popular Filipino street snack, Balut, is a fertilized duck egg, with a partially formed foetus inside. It is usually eaten by cracking open the shell and drinking the fluid. The foetus is then seasoned with salt and pepper, and eaten raw. Revered as an aphrodisiac, I can't imagine anything more likely to rid me of any passionate inclination.

ESCAMOLES

Harvested from giant black ant colonies at the roots of the agave plant in Mexico, Escamoles are ant eggs. The eggs are collected just before the larvae turn into ants, and the larvae collectors must wear protective clothes to guard against stings. They are said to taste like corn, have the texture of cottage cheese, and are often eaten in tacos.

HAKARL

An Icelandic dish, Hakarl is shark meat that has been cleaned and gutted in the normal way, then buried in gravel for up to four months. The fluids leave the shark flesh, putrefaction sets in, and the resultant meat smells – and tastes – like ammonia or stagnant urine. While eating it is said to be associated with Icelandic hardiness and strength, many people have a job keeping the meat down.

DURIAN

Native to south east Asia, durian fruit are about the size of the average melon. Known locally as the 'King of Fruits', they have a thorny, hard, light-green skin and sectioned yellow flesh. The odour of the flesh is described as being akin to smelly feet, or rotting flesh. Indeed it is so offensive that it is illegal to eat the durian in many public areas around Asia. Cooked as a sweet and a vegetable, the durian is prized for its medicinal uses and its high concentrations of various minerals and carbohydrates.

More Vegetables

POTATOES

These versatile staples fall into two broad categories:

* Waxy potatoes, such as Charlotte or Jersey Royals, have a high water, low starch content and keep their shape better when cooking, so they are ideal for boiling and using in salads.

* Floury potatoes, such as King Edwards or Maris Pipers, have a low water, high starch content, and become 'floury' when cooked, making them ideal for mashed or baked potatoes.

COOK'S TIP

To successfully reheat leftover baked potatoes, dip them in water, then bake them at 180°C/350°F until they are heated through.

When choosing potatoes, always look for a firm, smooth unblemished skin and avoid any with green patches or eyes. The nutrients in potatoes are found in or just beneath their skin, so if you have to peel them, don't take too much off.

* Store potatoes in a cool, dark well-ventilated place – but not in the fridge.

* Take potatoes out of plastic packaging as the humidity will cause mould.

* In general, floury potatoes can be stored for longer than waxy ones, although the longer potatoes are stored, the more nutritional value they'll lose.

COOK'S TIP

Don't store potatoes and onions together as they each give off gases that can cause decay in the other.
To keep potatoes from sprouting, add a few apples to your potato basket.

ROOT VEGETABLES

Carrots, swede, turnips, parsnips, beetroot, celeriac, radishes, all these vegetables have their own unique flavours and uses and they are all highly nutritious. When choosing them, always look for unblemished skins, with good colour and no soft spots or decay. Turnips and swede should feel firm and heavy for their size.

* Store in a cool, dry place, or in the fridge in a paper bag.

Large, naked, raw carrots are acceptable as food only to those who live in hutches eagerly awaiting Easter.

FRAN LEBOWITZ

✳ Take the tops off carrots, parsnips and radishes before storing, in order to prevent them from rotting.

Did you know?
A single carrot contains a whole day's recommended supply of vitamin A.

COOK'S TIP

Never store apples and carrots together. Apart from the ethylene emitted by the apples, they can also give carrots a bitter taste.

LEAFY GREENS

Full of goodness and taste, even though they are usually the most hated members of the vegetable family, leafy greens are the stars in the vegetable world. With spinach, sorrel, spring greens, kale, broccoli, cauliflower, cabbage, bok choy and the wonderful Brussels sprout (to name but a few), there's a world of flavour to enjoy and experiment with. Many of these vegetables are good sources of vitamins A, B and C, folates, iron, potassium and calcium, and the less they are cooked, the

> **COOK'S TIP**
>
> *To keep cauliflower white, boil it upside down, stalk uppermost, to prevent the scum that forms when boiling this vegetable from discolouring the 'flower'.*

more vitamins and minerals they'll retain. All these vegetables are best steamed.

* Try not to store any of these vegetables for too long – they need to be eaten fresh to retain their vibrant colours and taste.

* Some leafy greens, such as spinach, lose a great deal of their volume when cooked, so it's better to cook by weight rather than bulk.

> **COOK'S TIP**
>
> *To freshen up tired, wilted leafy vegetables, soak them in water with a splash of vinegar.*

PODS, SEEDS AND BEANS

Mangetouts, sugar snaps, garden peas, petit pois, sweetcorn, these are among the sweetest and most tasty vegetables, and need little preparation (sometimes none at all). Best eaten when they are fresh, young and tender, while peas are podded to remove the edible seed, mangetout and sugar snaps are eaten pod and all. Large cobs of sweetcorn do need to be cooked, but baby sweetcorn is perfect for enjoying in its natural state. When choosing vegetables from this group, try to buy them on the day you want to eat them. In all cases, try not to overcook these tender young things – they are all fantastic in stir-fries, and peas, mangetouts, sugar snaps and baby sweetcorn are delicious raw in salads.

French beans, runner beans, green beans and broad beans all need to be cooked. When choosing them, look for good colour and firm texture. If your green beans 'snap' crisply when you bend them, this is a good indicator of freshness.

* Store peas (in their pods) and other pods in the fridge until you need them – but try to use within 2 days. Likewise, sweetcorn is best eaten fresh and should not be stored for too long – 1 to 2 days maximum.

* Store beans in the fridge for 2 to 4 days.

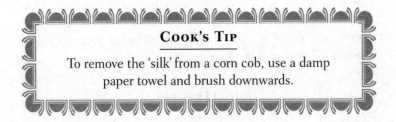

COOK'S TIP

To remove the 'silk' from a corn cob, use a damp paper towel and brush downwards.

Did you know?

Broad beans must always be cooked, as they can induce favism, a medical condition caused by enzyme deficiency in the blood that can lead to anaemia. On the upside, however, broad beans are a good source of protein, fibre and beta-carotene, iron, niacin and vitamins C and E.

Six
Celebrated Salads

SALAD NIÇOISE

Tuna fish, anchovies, tomatoes, cucumber, potatoes, green beans, black olives, capers and lettuce, served with a garlic vinaigrette dressing. The name 'Niçoise' relates to the ingredients most popularly used by the chefs of the city of Nice in the south of France.

CAESAR SALAD

Romaine lettuce with croutons, Parmesan cheese, anchovies, olive oil, garlic, lemon juice, raw egg and Worcestershire sauce. Said to originate in 1924 in honour of restaurateur Caesar Cardini in Tijuana, Mexico.

RUSSIAN SALAD

Cooked diced potatoes, peas, carrots and green beans mixed together with mayonnaise and served on a bed of lettuce along with hard-boiled eggs and pickles. Believed to be the creation of a French chef – Monsieur Olivier – who ran the Hermitage restaurant in Moscow in the 1860s. Also known as Olivier salad.

WALDORF SALAD

Apples, lemon juice, celery, raisins and walnuts all mixed together with mayonnaise. Believed to have been created in 1893 by Oscar Michel Tschirky, the *maitre d'* of New York's Waldorf Astoria.

COBB SALAD

Chicken or turkey with bacon, hard-boiled eggs, cheese, avocado, tomatoes and lettuce, served with a blue cheese vinaigrette dressing. It was invented in 1937 by Bob Cobb of the Brown Derby restaurant in Los Angeles.

PANZANELLA

A bread salad of Italian origin, panzanella also includes tomatoes, peppers, cucumber, onions, garlic, capers, black olives and anchovies. It is believed that this salad was created several centuries ago in order to use up stale bread.

Four Classic Sauces

BUTTER SAUCES

Both Hollandaise and Béarnaise sauce are known as 'butter sauces' because they are based on an emulsion of egg yolk and butter. Served warm with asparagus or eggs Benedict, you really can't beat a good Hollandaise, while the stronger flavoured Béarnaise is perfect with steaks.

Hollandaise

You will need:

3 egg yolks
3 tablespoons hot water
175 g (6 oz) unsalted butter
juice of ½ lemon
salt and pepper to taste

Whisk the egg yolks and water together in a heavy-based saucepan over a very low heat. In another saucepan, melt the butter over a very low heat, so that the butter solids fall to the bottom of the saucepan. When the butter is melted, gently add the butter to the egg mixture, a little at a time and whisking vigorously after each addition, taking care to leave the butter solids in the bottom of the saucepan. As the sauce thickens, whisk in the lemon juice and season to taste with salt and pepper.

You can add different flavours to a basic Hollandaise – try adding a tablespoon of Dijon mustard for a sauce Dijonnaise.

Béarnaise

You will need:

3 tablespoons tarragon vinegar
4 black peppercorns, crushed
1 large shallot, finely chopped
2 tablespoons fresh tarragon leaves, chopped
3 egg yolks
175g (6oz) unsalted butter, melted
salt
freshly ground black pepper

Boil the vinegar, peppercorns, shallot and tarragon until reduced by one third. Remove from the heat, add the egg yolks and whisk together. Return to a very low heat and whisk for three minutes, then beat in the melted butter a little at a time. Add salt and pepper to taste and serve warm.

COOK'S TIP

If your Béarnaise or Hollandaise separates or curdles (usually because the pan is too hot or the butter is added too quickly), take the pan off the heat, add an ice cube and whisk the sauce quickly, drawing more liquid in to the whisk as the ice cube melts.

ROUX SAUCES

A roux sauce is a mixture of butter and flour, and perhaps the white béchamel sauce is the best-known example. For a classic béchamel, the milk should be infused with sliced shallot, cloves, a bay leaf and freshly grated nutmeg before adding to the butter and flour mixture, but the recipe given here is for a basic white sauce, to which other flavourings can be added. A velouté sauce is made by the same method, but uses stock instead of milk.

White roux sauce

You will need:

> *15g (½oz) butter*
> *15g (½oz) flour*
> *300ml (10 floz) milk*
> *salt and pepper*

In a heavy-based saucepan, melt the butter over a low heat and add the flour. Using a wooden spoon, stir the mixture together briskly. Remove the pan from the heat and gradually add a little of the milk, stirring constantly to blend it with the butter and flour mixture. Continue to add the milk slowly and bring the mixture to a boil, stirring constantly over the whole base of the pan to prevent lumps forming. Lower the heat and simmer gently until the sauce has thickened. Season to taste.

Velouté

You will need:

> *1 litre stock or poaching liquid*
> *55g (2oz) butter*
> *55g (2oz) flour*
> *salt and pepper*

In a large saucepan, bring the stock or poaching liquid to a simmer. In a separate saucepan, melt the butter over a low heat and add the flour, stirring together with a wooden spoon, for 2 to 3 minutes. Remove from the heat and very gradually add the stock or poaching liquid, stirring constantly and bringing in the butter and flour mixture all the time. Bring to a boil, stirring constantly, then lower the heat and simmer, skimming off the thin skin that will form, for about 12 minutes. Season to taste.

COOK'S TIP

You can make many classic sauces from the basic velouté. Try adding about 150 ml (5 fl oz) freshly squeezed orange juice for a citrus sauce, or lemon juice and chopped fresh parsley for a meunière sauce.

Cook's Tips

* From this basic white roux sauce you can add ingredients such as cheese, parsley or mushrooms to create your favourite sauces to add to dishes such as lasagne and soufflés.

* The crucial thing with these sauces is the stirring, and a sauce that hasn't been stirred enough will become lumpy. If this happens, the best thing to do is to transfer the contents of the saucepan to a bowl and beat with a balloon whisk until the sauce becomes smooth again. Then strain it through a fine sieve back into the saucepan to reheat.

How to Eat 'Difficult' Food

It's always tricky when you're at a dinner party or in a restaurant and faced with something that you're not quite sure how to eat – fingers or cutlery? Here are a few examples of these foods and the 'correct' way they in which they should be eaten.

VEGETABLES

* Artichokes – with your fingers, take off the leaves one by one and dip the base of the leaf into the sauce provided. You then use your teeth to strip the flesh from the leaf and discard the woody inedible part at the side of your plate. The leaves nearest the artichoke heart have no flesh, so strip them off to expose the central core, scrape away the 'choke' (the thistly, fuzzy material), and eat the rest of the heart with your knife and fork.

* Asparagus – with your fingers, pick up each spear and dip it into the sauce provided. Eat as much of the spear as you can, but leave the woody end of the stem at the side of your plate.

* Corn on the cob – the cob, with a knob of butter already melting on it, may be served with small 'handles' inserted into each end. Use these to pick the cob up

and nibble away at the corn. If the corn is served
without handles, use your fingers. Whichever way you
do it, have a napkin at the ready.

SEAFOOD

* Crab – the meat will have been prepared and replaced
  in the shell. The claws may be served with a tool that
  looks like a nutcracker to crack them open and a metal
  pick with which to prise out the meat from within.

* Lobster – always a messy business, lobster is usually
  served cut in half lengthways. You will be provided with
  an implement with which to extract the meat from the
  claws, along with a finger bowl and, hopefully, an extra
  napkin.

* Mussels – when the steaming bowl of mussels arrives,
  select a large empty shell and use it like a pair of
  tweezers to pull the mussels from their shells. You
  should be provided with a separate bowl for empty
  shells and a finger bowl in which to rinse your fingers as
  you eat. Use a spoon to eat the stock.

* Prawns – when faced with large whole prawns, use your
  fingers to pull off the head, detaching it completely and
  discarding it in a separate bowl. Then turn the prawn
  over and peel away the shell, also removing the egg sac
  and legs. After detaching the tail shell, the body ought
  to be clean enough to eat. You should be provided with
  a separate bowl for empty shells and a finger bowl in
  which to rinse your fingers as you eat.

* Oysters – with a small fork, check that the oyster is detached from the half-shell, squeeze a little lemon juice over it and 'drink' the oyster, letting it slide into your mouth. Some people chew the oyster, others prefer to let it run straight down their throat.

* Whitebait – don't even try to fillet whitebait – these little fishes are cooked and eaten whole – eyes, tail, the lot.

OTHER FOODS

* Soup – as you eat soup, push the spoon away from you and sip from the spoon, never putting the whole spoon into your mouth. As you finish the soup, always tip the bowl away from you.

* Spaghetti – another potentially messy business, the trick is to put a fork into the spaghetti, so that the tines touch the base of the plate, and start to wind the pasta around the fork until a ball begins to form. Then take a spoon and tuck it under the forked spaghetti, still twisting the fork, and eat. As you eat from the fork, bite off any strands and let them fall back onto the plate.

* Cheese – when taking a slice of cheese from a cheeseboard, never cut a 'wedge' shape from the tip of the cheese, instead, cut along the length, leaving the cheese in a similar shape.

FRUIT

* Apple – first cut the apple into quarters, then core and peel individual pieces.

* Banana – using a knife, cut off both ends of the banana and then split the skin, peeling it away with your fingers. Using your dessert knife and fork, cut into small pieces and eat.

* Cherries – remove the stalk and eat whole, removing the stone discreetly between your thumb and index finger.

* Kiwi fruit – split in half width-wise and, using a teaspoon, scoop out the flesh to eat.

* Orange – using your dessert knife, score the skin in quarters and remove. Eat in segments.

* Pear – cut into quarters, then core and peel individual pieces. If a pear is very ripe, you could cut in half horizontally and scoop out the flesh with a teaspoon.

I have long believed that good food, good eating is all about risk. Whether we're talking about unpasteurized Stilton, raw oysters or working for organized crime 'associates', food, for me, has always been an adventure.

ANTHONY BOURDAIN, *Kitchen Confidential*

In Praise of the Humble Egg

No matter what you may have been told about how easy it is to cook an egg, there is an art to it and you can get perfect results every time if you follow a few simple rules.

COOK'S TIP

Fresh eggs sink in a bowl of cool, salted water, whereas bad eggs will float on the surface.

BOILED EGGS

* First rule: never 'boil' an egg. Eggs benefit from being cooked in water just below boiling point.

✳ Putting your egg in cold water and bringing to a gentle simmer will help prevent the shell from breaking.

✳ Fresh eggs tend to crack more readily than older eggs. Adding a teaspoon of vinegar to the water when you are boiling an egg will lessen the chances of the eggs cracking, but if your egg does crack during boiling, adding a touch of vinegar will help to seal it.

✳ Turning your egg while it's simmering will help the yolk to set in the centre of the egg, which is important if you are serving the egg stuffed or decorating a salad.

Soft-boiled egg

For a medium-sized soft-cooked egg with a runny yolk and firm white, cook the egg for 2 to 3 minutes at simmering point. For a firmer white and a yolk that will stay in shape, cook for 2 to 3 minutes more.

Hard-boiled egg

A medium-sized hard-boiled egg should be cooked for 8 to 10 minutes at simmering point. If you plunge your egg into cold water immediately after cooking you will not get the nasty greenish/black ring that sometimes forms around the yolk.

COOK'S TIP

Use a wet knife to slice hard-boiled eggs.
This will help the white and yolk to stay together.

Scrambled eggs

For four people you will need:

> 8 medium-sized eggs
> freshly ground sea salt
> freshly ground black pepper
> 2 tablespoons butter

Break the eggs into a bowl and beat them with a fork until the whites and yolk are thoroughly blended together. Season to taste with sea salt and black pepper. Melt the butter in a heavy copper-bottomed pan or cast-iron skillet over a low heat and, before the butter begins to bubble, pour in the beaten egg. Use the bottom and sides of the pan to cook the egg, pulling the cooked egg in to the centre of the pan to allow the liquid egg to touch the base and sides. Using a flexible spatula, keep the egg moving around the pan at all times to prevent burning and aid the cooking process. When all the egg is becoming firm, remove the pan from the heat and, while the heat of the pan does the final cooking, scramble the eggs rapidly with a fork and serve immediately.

Poached egg

For the perfect breakfast egg you will need:

> 1 litre (1¾ pints) water
> 1 tablespoon vinegar
> 1 egg

Bring the water and vinegar to a boil and turn down the heat to simmering point. Break the egg into a cup. Using a spoon, turn circles in the water to create a 'whirlpool', and drop the egg gently into the centre of the whirlpool. Poach for about 3 minutes or until the white is set. Using a slotted spoon, remove the egg from the water, trim off any straggly white and serve with a pile of warm toast.

Fried eggs

For many, the fried egg is the most difficult to get right. The crowning glory on any Full English Breakfast, it can be infuriating when the fried egg is just not good enough! The secret, I think, is in using a frying pan with a lid.

For two people you will need:

> *1 tablespoon butter*
> *2 large eggs*
> *salt*
> *freshly ground black pepper*

Place a small heavy-bottomed frying pan (with a lid) on the hob over a low heat and add the butter. Let it melt slowly, but don't let it foam. Meanwhile, crack each egg into a small cup and gently slide each egg into the frying pan. Cover the pan with the lid. How quickly the egg cooks depends on the strength of the heat underneath it, but the eggs should cook for about 5 minutes until the white solidifies and the yolk thickens. When your egg is cooked, slide it onto a serving plate and season with salt and pepper.

> *But doth not the appetite alter? A man loves the meat in his youth that he cannot endure in his age.*
>
> **WILLIAM SHAKESPEARE**
> *Much Ado About Nothing*

Seafood

Many people say they 'don't like' fish and seafood, when what they really mean is that they don't like handling and preparing fish and seafood, which can be quite fiddly. The thing is, the fiddling *is* worth it, so here are a few tips and techniques for making the most of the fish you buy.

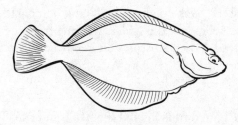

CHOOSING FISH

There are four categories of seafood – seawater fish, freshwater fish, preserved fish and shellfish, and all should be eaten as fresh as possible. Freshwater fish should smell clean, while seawater fish should smell of the sea.

Four clues to freshness:

* skin should be shiny and damp to the touch, and any natural markings or colourings should be bright not dull or dimmed

* body should be firm and smooth not limp and floppy

* gills should be clean and bright with no traces of slime

* eyes should be full and moist not dull or cloudy

PREPARING FISH

Trimming and scaling

Both round fish, which includes salmon and trout, and flat fish, such as plaice, sole or turbot, need to be trimmed and have the scales removed before cooking.

* Trim all the fins off the fish with a pair of kitchen scissors.

* Using the back of a large knife and holding the tail firmly, scrape off the scales, working from the tail to the head. When all scales are removed, rinse under running water.

Gutting

Flat fish are gutted from behind the head, and usually at sea, so you won't have to do this. However the easiest way to gut round fish is through the stomach (actually the easiest way is to get your fishmonger to do it for you, but here's how to do it, just in case).

* Having trimmed and scaled the fish (see above), cut out the gills under the fish's head, then make a small slice at the bottom of the stomach and cut straight along the underside of the fish, stopping just below the gills.

* Using your hands, take hold of the fish's innards, pull them out and discard them.

* Run a tablespoon along the inside of the gutted fish, against each side of its backbone, to get rid of any blood vessels, which can make the fish taste bitter when cooked.

✻ Rinse the inside of the fish thoroughly under cold running water, and now it's ready for cooking.

COOK'S TIP

Beware overcooking fish – if it's cooked for too long the fish will become tough and dry. To test fish for doneness, press gently with the tip of a knife. The fish is cooked when the flesh has turned opaque and the flakes separate easily.

Skinning flat fish and round fillets

Flat fish swim on their sides, with both eyes on the top of their body. The 'top' skin of a flat fish is dark, in order to camouflage the fish from its predators at sea. If you are serving the fish whole, you only need to remove the dark top skin as the white under skin will help hold the fish's shape during cooking.

✻ Using a small sharp knife, scrape the dark skin away from the tail to loosen it from the flesh.

✻ Take a firm hold of the skin in one hand and the flesh in the other and pull the skin away from the tail, working it down the whole body and detaching it completely from the fish. With a firm movement, it should come off completely in one go.

COATINGS AND BATTERS

Try these ideas for coatings and batters when frying fish – they will keep the fillets moist while cooking and are both subtle and tasty, enhancing the fish's natural flavours.

* Blend together paprika, onion powder and garlic powder, dried thyme and oregano, cayenne pepper, black pepper and salt and rub over the fish fillet before frying.

* Mix together fragrant fresh herbs such as chopped dill, crushed fennel seeds and coarsely ground black pepper.

* Mix chopped chives and some grated lemon zest into fine breadcrumbs or flour.

* When making batter, use beer instead of milk for a light and tasty coating.

* Try flavouring your batter flour with chilli or curry powder.

COOK'S TIP

To make it less slippery and difficult to handle, rinse your fish in hot water to which a little vinegar has been added and rub the skin. Pat the fish dry with kitchen paper.

CHOOSING SHELLFISH

✳ Prawns – avoid any prawns (cooked or fresh) with black spots. Make sure they look bright in colour and smell fresh.

✳ Oysters – the shells must be tightly closed and undamaged and they should smell fresh and briny.

✳ Lobsters and crabs – if buying live, look for an active lobster or crab and choose one that feels heavy for its size; if buying cooked, make sure the shell is undamaged and the claws intact.

✳ Scallops – these are usually sold opened and cleaned rather than in their shells. Make sure they smell fresh.

✳ Mussels, clams and cockles – avoid those that are covered in barnacles or that appear cracked or damaged, and discard any that remain open when tapped.

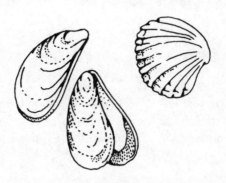

COOK'S TIP

One of my favourite ways of cooking trout is to bake it in newspaper. Take a good, fresh trout, trimmed, scaled, gutted and washed, and wrap it tightly in a page of your favourite newspaper (a single page of a broadsheet, but a double-page spread from a tabloid). Soak the newspaper in cold water under the tap, then place in a pre-heated oven at 190°C/375°F/Gas Mark 5 for 20 minutes.

Take the parcel out and place it on a work surface. Using kitchen scissors, cut the parcel open from one end of the fish and gently ease the paper away from the cooked trout. The skin will come off with the newspaper and you will have a simple, delicious and skin-free fish to enjoy.

Spice It Up!

There's nothing like a touch of spice when it comes to imparting aroma and added flavour to your dish. Here are a few pointers on what spices go with what.

* Allspice – use in Christmas puddings and biscuits, but also in pickles and marinades. Buy the whole spice to grind at home if possible, as the flavour of ready-ground spice fades rapidly.

* Anise – use in sweet and savoury dishes. Good in cakes, biscuits and kneaded into the dough when making breads. Buy whole seeds to grind at home.

* Caraway – use in vegetable dishes and soups and in cakes, biscuits and breads. Ground caraway has a very intense flavour, so use sparingly and use whole seeds where possible.

* Cardamom – use in curries, pilaffs, dhals and for cakes and desserts. Widely used in Indian sweet and savoury dishes. Use the green or white cardamom pods only, the brown pods are strong and overpowering.

* Cinnamon – used mainly in sweet dishes, cakes and biscuits, but also good in poultry and game dishes.

* Celery seeds – use in sauces and soups, casseroles and stews, egg dishes, with fish and poultry. Also a wonderful addition to a Bloody Mary.

✳ Cloves – use in sweet and savoury dishes, Christmas cakes and puddings, with stewed fruit, in bread sauce, in pickles and marinades and in stews.

COOK'S TIP

For extra flavour, stud two or three cloves into an onion and use when making bread sauce or chicken stock or for any slow-cooked casserole.
Don't use too many cloves, though, as the flavour will take over the whole dish.

✳ Coriander seeds – use ground seeds in curries and in meat, poultry and vegetable dishes. Use whole seeds in pickles and chutneys. Buy whole and grind at home.

✳ Cumin – use in curries (cumin is a key ingredient in garam masala), Mexican dishes, with couscous and in meat casseroles. Buy whole and grind at home.

✳ Dill seeds – use crushed seeds in fish and egg dishes, with potatoes and as a flavouring for home-made mayonnaise and in vinegar. Can be used whole or crushed in pickles.

✳ Fennel seeds – use whole or crushed seeds in breads and biscuits. Ground fennel seeds are used in curries and in meat dishes.

✳ Fenugreek – great in meat, poultry, fish or vegetable curries, but use sparingly as the flavour is strong.

* Ginger – used in savoury dishes throughout Asia in meat, poultry and fish dishes, in curries, in marinades and in salad dressings and in pickles; also used in sweet dishes, ice creams, cakes and tarts.

* Mace – use in béchamel and onion sauces, with shellfish, cheese soufflés and in cream cheese desserts. Mace and nutmeg come from the same tree but mace gives a slightly lighter flavour.

* Nutmeg – fragrant and warming, use nutmeg in cakes, puddings and milk sauces; in pasta dishes and with vegetables, poultry and fish dishes.

* Paprika – use in potato, rice and noodle dishes, for goulash, with veal or poultry. Often used in Spanish, Hungarian and Turkish cookery.

COOK'S TIP

Ginger keeps very well in the freezer. Every time you need fresh ginger, grate the desired amount and put the rest back in the freezer.

* Saffron – a very singular flavour, saffron is great in soups, goes well in fish, egg and rice dishes, and cakes, breads and biscuits.

Cook's Tip

To release the flavour of saffron, you must soak it first. Place a few threads in warm water or milk for about 10 minutes, stirring occasionally. Then stir the threads – and the liquid – into the dish you're preparing.

* Star anise – use in chicken and duck dishes and with fish and shellfish; star anise is used widely in Chinese cooking.

* Tamarind – use in curries, vegetable dishes and in pickles.

* Turmeric – used in curries, in fish, poultry and rice dishes and in pickles, turmeric (also known as Indian saffron) is a very popular Indian spice.

Cook's Tip

When making curries, heat your curry powder up in the oven for five minutes before adding it to the dish. This will make the flavour more pungent.

✳ Vanilla – use in desserts, ice creams, and custards. Always go for vanilla extract (made from the spice) rather than vanilla essence.

Too spicy?

To cut spiciness, add more of everything else the recipe calls for. The three things that counteract spice are acids, dairy and sugar, so try a few squirts of lemon or lime juice. If appropriate, you could add yogurt, sour cream, cream or coconut milk. Lastly, granulated or brown sugar may help.

> *Once you get a spice in your home, you have it forever. Women never throw out spices. The Egyptians were buried with their spices. I know which one I am taking with me when I go.*
>
> **ERMA BOMBECK**

Even More Vegetables

SQUASHES

These are classified into summer and winter squashes. Summer squashes, such as courgettes, are more tender and even have soft, edible skins, whereas winter squashes, such as spaghetti squash, are tougher skinned and need to be peeled and have their seeds removed. When choosing, always look for hard, blemish-free skin and a fresh, bright colour. Try a few different pumpkins and squashes if you can, they all have distinctive flavours and are great accompaniments for stews and casseroles as well as delicious soups. It's worth remembering that squashes are good sources of vitamins A and C, and contain calcium, iron and potassium.

* The bigger summer squashes can be stored at room temperature for about a week or in the fridge for a few weeks, but some, like courgettes and pattypan squashes, need to be eaten when they are fresh.

* The thicker-skinned winter squashes can keep well for a lot longer. Store in a cool, dry place for several months.

* When cooking butternut squash or pumpkin, save yourself the trouble of peeling it by cutting it into sections, scooping out the seeds and stringy fibres and cooking it in its skin. When it's cooked, scoop out the flesh.

PEPPERS AND CHILLIES

Peppers should feel firm and have a shiny, unblemished skin. Chillies often have wrinkly skin even though they are fresh. A general rule is that the smaller the chilli, the hotter it is (see pages 37–39).

* Store peppers in a cool place such as the chiller compartment of the fridge for a few days.

* Chillies can be placed in a plastic bag in the chiller compartment and will keep for about two weeks.

* Dried chillies are often used as a substitute for fresh. To rehydrate them simply soak them for an hour in a bowl of warm water, then grind them into a paste and press through a fine sieve to remove the skins.

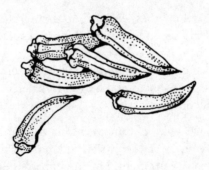

Be careful!
Always be careful when preparing chillies as the volatile oil they contain, capsaicin, can burn skin and eyes. Either wear rubber gloves when preparing them or make sure you wash your hands thoroughly after preparation.

TOMATOES

When choosing tomatoes check that they are firm and brightly coloured. They should 'give' slightly when pressure is applied. Tomatoes left on the vine to ripen will have more flavour and are worth the extra money they cost.

* Store under-ripe tomatoes at room temperature in a dark place or brown paper bag, as storing in the fridge can stop the ripening process and destroy the flavour. Once fully ripe, store tomatoes in the fridge but try to eat within 1 to 2 days as their flavour will deteriorate.

* To ripen green tomatoes (or unripe peaches or pears), store them in a paper bag along with an apple and leave them in a cool, dark place. The ethylene gas from the apple hastens the ripening process.

* To de-skin tomatoes, either drop them in boiling water for 30 seconds then peel, or stick a fork in the tomato, hold it over the gas ring and let the skin blacken and blister. When you take the tomato away from the heat source and off the fork you'll find the skin will come off easily.

* If you have a glut of tomatoes from the garden, remember they can be frozen – skin on or off – if you plan to cook with them. Lay the tomatoes on a tray and put the tray in the freezer for 45 minutes. Place the semi-frozen tomatoes in a freezer bag and put them back in the freezer. They will keep for up to 3 months and, once defrosted, although not suitable to be eaten raw, will be very useful for soups and stews.

Wine with Food

The old adage white with fish, red with meat just doesn't quite cut it anymore. We are now faced with so much choice in the supermarket that it can be quite boggling trying to decide which wine would go best with your forthcoming Sunday lunch or dinner party. Of course, when you're simply pleasing yourself you know what you like, but when it comes to choosing the best wine to go with particular dishes, your choice can make a marked difference to the flavours both of the wine and the food served, so here are a few general suggestions for savouries to get you started.

MEAT

* Beef – every meat has its own distinctive flavour, and how you cook it make a difference to how that flavour manifests itself on your palate. If you're serving a simple rump steak, you'll need a robust red wine like a Bordeaux to accentuate the beefy flavours of the meat, whereas if you have a beef casserole in mind you might try a milder, lighter Burgundy.

* Lamb – the deep rich flavours of a Bordeaux bring out the flavours in older lamb dishes, while a Grenache is often perfect with roast spring lamb.

* Pork – for roast pork, a full-bodied Rioja will go down well, whereas a Chianti might be more suitable for marinated or barbecued pork.

* Cold meats – preserved meats such as salami need a rich red wine to cut through their very strong flavours, so go for a Pinot Noir or a wine from the Rhone valley.

* Veal – the whiter the meat, the lighter the wine should be, so often white wines such as Vouvray or Soave are very good served with white veal. For darker meat, a rich Bordeaux will bring out the flavour well.

FISH

* Freshwater fish – trout or salmon need fresh white wines to accentuate their natural flavours, so try a Chablis or light-bodied Reisling to bring those flavours out.

* Seawater fish – haddock, cod and other seawater fish are best served simply poached with a squeeze of lemon. Try a Chardonnay or a White Burgundy to bring out the lemony fresh flavours.

* Smoked and oily fish – of course, for smoked salmon Champagne is the best partner, but if smoked mackerel is on your menu, try a light, crisp Mosel to cut through that strong flavour. For the meaty textures and flavours of tuna, sardines and mackerel, go for a sturdy Muscadet or even a fruity Beaujolais to complement the fish.

* Shellfish – lobster, crab, prawns, shrimp, there's a great variety of shellfish and your choice of wine will depend on how you're cooking them. A fruity Gewurztraminer will be lovely with simply prepared lobster, or crab, whereas you might find a spicy red Rioja will go perfectly with shrimp or prawns cooked in a creamy sauce.

POULTRY

* Chicken – a classic roast chicken is well complimented either by a crisp Chablis or, for the darker meat, a young red such as Shiraz.

* Turkey – richer-tasting than chicken, turkey needs a fuller-bodied wine to reveal its flavours, so go for a Shiraz or try a fruity Zinfandel.

* Duck – rich and distinctive in flavour, this bird needs a rich red wine such as Rhone or Burgundy to compliment it.

VEGETARIAN DISHES

* Pasta – for dishes such as lasagne or pasta bakes, it has to be a Chianti.

* Rice – if you're serving a creamy risotto, make sure the wine you serve with it is light and crisp – like a Pinot Grigio – to cut through the creaminess.

* Vegetables, nut and bean dishes – for a simple dish of roast vegetables, you can either try a full-bodied Merlot or go for a well-balanced and softer Rosé.

Foods to Forage for

From moor, meadow and woodland, there are lots of foods to be found for free, many of which are prized for their health-giving properties. If you do go foraging, don't strip a plant of all its berries or leaves, take a few from several plants so that the plant stays healthy, and always make sure you wash your pickings before enjoying them.

* Bilberries – these tart little berries ripen in the late summer and are great in pies and fools or made into jam. Bilberry tart is a traditional dessert in south-central France.

* Blackberries – ripening from late August, blackberries are a good source of vitamin C and dietary fibre. Avoid fruits growing on busy roadsides and always wash the fruit you pick. Blackberry leaf tea is used as a gargle for sore throats in natural medicine.

* Dandelions – available most of the year, the fresh young leaves have a slightly bitter flavour and taste fantastic in a green salad. A good source of beta carotene, calcium, potassium and loaded with iron, the French call this plant *pissenlit*, 'wet the bed', because of its diuretic qualities.

* Sloes – best picked after the first frosts, the dark blue sloe berry is small and very bitter to taste, but my mother-in-law's sloe gin, always ready in time for Christmas, is fantastic – in small quantities. You can also use sloes to make a clear jelly as a meat accompaniment.

* Stinging nettles – best picked in the spring (and wearing gloves), stinging nettles are a good source of beta carotene, vitamin C, calcium, iron and potassium. Rinse the nettles and discard any tough stalks, then steam. Nettles lose their sting when cooked and can be used in quiches or soups as an alternative to spinach. In natural medicine, like dandelions, nettles are a natural diuretic and are also believed to help eczema sufferers. Don't pick nettles from the roadside – they may have had herbicides used on them.

* Wild chicory – the ragged leaves that are similar to cultivated chicory or endive can be added to salads for the familiar bitter taste. Wild chicory is a good source of beta carotene, vitamin C and potassium.

* Wild garlic – found in damp woodland, usually near bluebells. Its long leaves are similar to lily of the valley, but you'll be able to tell if you've found it by its unmistakable smell.

* Wild rose – the small orange rose-hips usually appear in late August and are packed with vitamin C. Rose-hips can be stewed and added to pies, tarts, etc., but make sure you sieve the stewed fruit before using it to get rid of the spiny hairs around the seeds.

* Wild strawberries – the fantastic fresh taste of summer, strawberries are said to cleanse the digestive system and relieve joint pain. As for cooking with them, you'll be lucky to get them home!

DOS AND DON'TS OF FORAGING

* Don't allow children to forage unless accompanied by an adult.

* Don't pick near busy roads, where the soil and plants may be contaminated by fumes.

* Don't forage for food near cultivated crops that may have been sprayed with chemicals.

* Don't pick *anything* you are unsure of.

* Do obey 'no trespassing' signs, no matter what delicacy you have your eye on.

* Do your research and make sure you know what you're looking for and looking at. Take a well-illustrated book with you when you forage.

Nettle broth

Use fresh young nettles in this satisfying recipe.
To serve 4 you will need:

knob of butter
1 medium onion, finely chopped
600 ml (1 pint) chicken stock
50 g (1¾ oz) pearl barley
300 g (10½ oz) nettles, washed and finely chopped
salt and pepper to taste

Melt the butter in a heavy-based saucepan and add the onion. When the onion is translucent, pour in the stock. Rinse and drain the barley and add to the stock. Bring to a boil slowly, then stir in the finely chopped nettles and simmer very gently until the barley is tender. Season to taste.

In the Dairy

The general term 'dairy products' applies to all items derived from milk – be it cow's, goat's or sheep's – and there are some tricks to be aware of when cooking with foods from this group.

MILK

Although most milk is consumed in drinks, both milk and cream are very important ingredients in many recipes, from sauces to desserts. Milk doesn't freeze well (and should only be used for cooking with after freezing) and must be stored in the fridge, where it will keep for 3 to 4 days.

Cook's Tip

When warming milk, to help prevent it from boiling over, and to lessen the amount of milk sticking to the pan when you've finished, rinse the pan in cold running water first.

CREAM

The basic ingredient and 'crowning glory' of many desserts, cream also adds richness and depth to stews, soups and pasta dishes. As with cheese, the key to successful cooking with cream is to look at its fat content. Cream with a higher fat content is more 'stable', easier to whip and less likely to curdle when cooking.

* Single cream contains the lowest amount of fat – 18 per cent – so it can't be used for whipping but is useful for adding to desserts or giving body to soups, casseroles or sauces.

* Whipping cream has a much higher fat content – 38 per cent – but it is a lighter alternative to double cream in cooking. Whipping cream will whip up to twice its original volume, and can be piped onto cakes, trifles and other cold desserts. Try using it in a mousse for a lighter texture.

* Double cream is 48 per cent fat, and as such is the most stable and versatile cream to use when cooking. It imparts richness and texture to all sorts of savoury and sweet dishes, from spooning over desserts to adding to sauces. You can whip it, pipe it or use it as a topping.

* Clotted cream – at 55 per cent fat, the fattiest of all our creams – is pale yellow, rich and thick. A Cornish cream tea with scones, jam and clotted cream is a real treat.

Cook's Tip

Take care when adding single cream to hot dishes. If it's too hot the cream will curdle, so let it cool slightly first. Equally, don't let single cream boil as this will also make it curdle.

COOK'S TIP

To make sour cream, stir a teaspoon of lemon juice
into about 250 ml (9 fl oz) double cream and allow it to
stand for 30 minutes or until it has thickened. Cover
and put in the fridge until ready to use.

All cream should be kept in the fridge and used within two to
three days. Apart from clotted cream, which can be frozen for
up to a month, other creams, in their 'raw' state, don't freeze
well. However double cream and whipping cream can be frozen
for a month if lightly whipped first.

Crème fraîche

You can buy this classic French product ready made, but it's
easy to make at home. Fantastic on strawberries, raspberries or
any summer fruits, and equally useful in savoury dishes, in
sauces or soups.

You will need:

250 ml (9 fl oz) buttermilk
125 ml (4 fl oz) double cream

Mix together the buttermilk and double cream and heat in a
heavy-based saucepan until it reaches body temperature (test it
with your finger, it should be just warm). Pour the mixture into
a glass bowl, cover and let it stand at room temperature
overnight. It will keep in the fridge for up to 5 days.

CHEESE

I love cheese, all types: hard, soft, blue, goat's – the lot, but there are certain cheeses that are better for cooking with than others. It's all to do with the cheese's fat and moisture content and how these react to heat. The trick is in picking the right cheese for your recipe.

> *Dinner without cheese is like a beautiful woman with only one eye.*
> **JEAN ANTHELME BRILLAT-SAVARIN**

Six good melting cheeses

* Mozzarella – an old favourite on pizza toppings, Mozzarella melts evenly and makes those wonderful strings of cheese.

* Cheddar – is fantastic for grilling as it melts evenly and browns well.

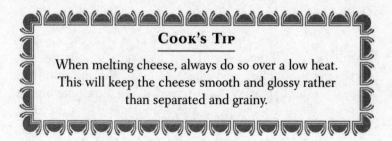

COOK'S TIP

When melting cheese, always do so over a low heat.
This will keep the cheese smooth and glossy rather
than separated and grainy.

✱ Gruyère – for gratin toppings, Gruyère can't be beaten. It
is best to grate the cheese before adding it to the dish and
placing under the grill to brown.

✱ Emmenthal – similar to Gruyère, Emmenthal is great as a
gratin topping or on quiches and bakes.

✱ Fontina – has a high melting point (it can even be deep-
fried in breadcrumbs and still keep its shape); lovely on
macaroni cheese.

✱ Goat's cheese – when grilled it holds its shape well and
has a fantastic consistency.

COOK'S TIP

To keep cheese fresh and free from mould, dampen a
piece of kitchen towel with vinegar and keep it in
your cheese box in the refrigerator.

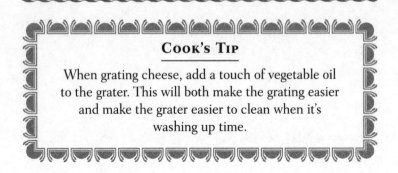

Cook's Tip

When grating cheese, add a touch of vegetable oil
to the grater. This will both make the grating easier
and make the grater easier to clean when it's
washing up time.

Perfect cheese sauce

Success lies in making a white sauce first (see page 80) and then
adding the grated cheese as the milk warms. Stir constantly and
evenly and don't whisk for a velvety sauce every time.

Microwave melting

You can use the microwave to melt small amounts of cheese
quickly. A 225 g (8 oz) block will take about a minute, but watch
out as ovens vary a great deal.

Storing cheese

Hard cheeses keep for longer than soft ones, but it's best to buy
cheese in small amounts and eat it quickly rather than keep it
for any length of time. Most cheeses can be frozen, but freezing
can affect the cheese's flavour and texture. Camembert,
Cheddar, Edam, Gouda, Mozzarella, Parmesan and blue
cheeses are fine in the freezer, but cream and cottage cheeses
don't freeze well. Wrap portions of fresh cheese in a layer of
cling-film then aluminium foil and freeze for up to three
months. Defrost cheese in the fridge for 24 hours.

STORING AND FREEZING DAIRY

Store dairy products in the fridge well away from meat products to lessen the chance of cross-contamination. If you have space in your fridge, it is best stored in a dedicated cheese drawer or airtight box.

Always observe the 'use-by' dates on dairy products, particularly milk and cream, and don't use those that are out-of-date. Milk can easily pick up aromas from the fridge, so it's best to buy it in containers that can be easily resealed. Tightly cover part-used cream with cling film and/or aluminium foil.

COOK'S TIP

If you store cheese in the fridge, make sure you take it out and let it 'warm up' to room temperature at least half an hour before serving – this way you will enjoy the cheese at its best.

Mayonnaise and Dressings

Mayonnaise

Nothing compares to the taste of home-made mayonnaise. Once you've mastered the technique you'll want to make it again and again.

You will need:

1 large egg yolk
1 tablespoon Dijon mustard
salt and freshly ground pepper
300 ml (10 fl oz) oil (half-and-half olive
and vegetable oil works well)
2 teaspoons white wine vinegar

Whisk the egg yolk, mustard and seasonings in a bowl and begin to add the oil, continuing to whisk the mixture until it is well blended in. Add more oil and whisk again, repeating this process until the sauce emulsifies and begins to thicken. Stop adding oil when the mayonnaise has reached the desired thickness. Whisk in the vinegar to taste.

Two methods of 'saving' home-made mayonnaise gone-wrong:

* By hand: mix one tablespoon of cold water or wine vinegar with a little of the curdled mayonnaise and gradually combine more mayonnaise as you go.

* By food processor: add one egg yolk to the curdled mixture and put the food processor on pulse until the mixture becomes creamy again.

Have all your ingredients and equipment at room
temperature when making mayonnaise. If the
ingredients are too cold the mixture may separate.

Mayonnaise by any other name

Try adding some different flavours to your mayonnaise.

* Add 4 crushed garlic cloves instead of the mustard.

* Add 2 crushed garlic cloves and 2 tablespoons of
finely chopped red pepper.

* Stir in finely chopped herbs, such as tarragon, parsley
or chervil.

* Add 2 teaspoons of curry powder to spice up an egg
dish.

> *Aïoli [garlic mayonnaise] epitomizes the heat,
> the power, and the joy of the Provençal sun,
> but it has another virtue – it drives away flies.*
>
> **FRÉDÉRIC MISTRAL**

DRESSINGS

The key ingredient in any dressing is the oil, so be sure to use the best quality to produce the best taste.

Vinaigrette

Traditionally made with three parts oil to one part vinegar, a classic vinaigrette is all a salad needs to bring out the flavours. Try to buy oils and vinegars that compliment each other for the best vinaigrette – nut oils, for example, pair well with fruit vinegars such as raspberry vinegar, while extra virgin olive oil pairs well with the tartness imparted by balsamic vinegar.

You will need:

2 tablespoons vinegar
2 teaspoons Dijon mustard
salt and freshly ground black pepper
6 tablespoons oil

Put the vinegar, mustard and seasonings into a small bowl and combine together. Slowly add the oil, whisking continuously until the dressing is smooth and thickened.

> ### COOK'S TIP
>
> When mixing oil and vinegar into a salad, add the oil first as if you lead with the vinegar the oil will slip off the lettuce and tomatoes and end up in the bottom of the bowl.

Flavour your vinaigrette

* Add zest with a little honey and lemon or lime juice.

* Add a little finely crushed ginger for a tangy bite.

* Add crushed toasted sesame seeds for a nutty flavour.

> *To make a good salad is to be a brilliant diplomat – the problem is entirely the same in both cases. To know how much oil to put with one's vinegar.*
>
> **OSCAR WILDE**

Nice Rice

A staple food around the world, rice is a nutritious complex carbohydrate and one of the most flexible foods, which can be served as an accompaniment with curries and casseroles, or the main part of the dish, as in risottos, pilaffs or rice salads. Often a big hit with children, combining rice with vegetables, fish and other foods can persuade kids to try something different.

TYPES OF RICE

White, brown, black, red, organic and wild rice – the varieties available are enormous, but each type of rice has its own special characteristics.

* Long-grain or American long-grain – this is the most commonly available rice. It generally comes from the USA because rice grown in China and the Far East is usually for home consumption.

* Basmati – aromatic and flavourful, basmati comes from the Punjab region of India.

* Jasmine rice – long-grain and fragrant, this is slightly stickier than basmati and is suitable for both sweet and savoury dishes.

* Risotto rice – arborio and carnaroli are the most commonly known types of this short-grained rice developed especially for the creamy Italian risotto.

* Paella rice – medium-grain rice such as Calasparra and Valencia are perfect for a true Spanish paella.

* Sushi rice – a white, short-grained and sticky rice perfect for sushi.

* Red rice – also known as Carmargue rice, this is semi-wild rice from that region of France. Similar to brown rice in that it has an earthy, nutty flavour.

* Wild rice – has a nutty flavour and firm texture.

WASHING RICE

Basmati and ordinary long-grain rice are improved if they are washed before cooking. Simply put the rice in a large bowl and cover with cold water. Stir the rice with your fingers and the water will become cloudy. Let the rice settle and gently tip the bowl over to drain away the cloudy water. Repeat this two or three more times until the water drains away clear.

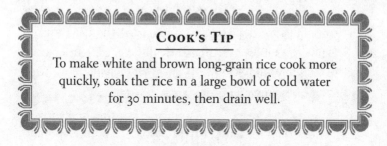

Cook's Tip

To make white and brown long-grain rice cook more quickly, soak the rice in a large bowl of cold water for 30 minutes, then drain well.

COOKING RICE

The three best ways of cooking rice are:

* In hot water – place the rice in a saucepan and add plenty of boiling water. Cook as per the packet

instructions, then drain through a colander or sieve. If the rice is to be served cold, you can rinse it to remove any excess starch.

* By absorption – cook your rice in a measured amount of water, usually 2 parts water to 1 part rice. The rice, cooked in a pan with a tightly fitted lid so that, in effect, it cooks in its own steam, is cooked when the water is completely absorbed, after about 15 minutes. Fluff up the grains with a fork.

* In the microwave – rice cooks well in the microwave. Just put your rice and boiling water into a bowl, cover with clingfilm and cook, as per the packet instructions. Allow the rice to stand for 10 minutes after cooking. Fluff up the grains with a fork.

COOK'S TIP

Did you know, apart from risotto, you're not meant to stir rice as it cooks? Apparently this can cause the grains to release extra starch and break.

RICE COOKERS

If you cook lots of rice it may be worth investing in an electric rice cooker, which basically uses the absorption method outlined above to cook perfect rice every time. These will also keep the rice warm after cooking, without it becoming soggy or too dry.

TIPS FOR THE PERFECT RISOTTO

* Use a heavy-based saucepan when you cook risotto, as this will retain the heat and keep the rice at a steady, gentle simmer.

* When adding the stock, do so very gradually, keeping the rice moist rather than drowning it in liquid.

* Stir, stir and stir again!

* Serve as soon as the risotto is cooked, as if it is left to stand, the risotto will continue to absorb liquid.

No one who cooks, cooks alone. Even at her most solitary, a cook in the kitchen is surrounded by generations of cooks past, the advice and menus of cooks present, the wisdom of cookbook writers.

LAURIE COLWIN

Make It Last!

PRESERVING FRUIT

There are so many fantastic and flavourful fruits around that it's a shame not to grab them in season and keep them for use throughout the year – or give specially preserved pots to friends as gifts. There are several methods you can use to simply keep the fruits, and a few that will make them extra special.

* Make a purée – cook your fruit in a little water and, when soft, purée the fruit then sieve it to remove any pips. Put a small amount of the fruit purée in an airtight container and freeze. When you need it, defrost, sweeten the purée to taste and use as a tasty sauce over ice cream, spooned over peaches or mixed into yogurt or in your recipe.

* Make jam – it's a more complicated process, but there's nothing to beat the taste of home-made jam,

and when you can forage for blackberries in the autumn (see page 108) you can really be the best cook ever! The basic principle is to use the same ratio of sugar to fruit pulp in jam making, but it's best to look for a recipe when you have your fruit, as some need extra pectin added.

* Make a conserve – these are usually made with large pieces of fruit, or whole fruits, suspended in a thick syrup. First the fruit is layered with an equal quantity of sugar (as in jam making), and left to stand for twenty-four hours. It is then boiled (again, as in jam making) but for a much shorter length of time, thus preserving the fruit close to its original state rather than in 'spreadable' form.

* Bottling fruit – preserve your fruit whole in syrup or alcohol for use with ice creams or in mousses or fools (see page 128).

* Freezing – spread berries onto a tray to freeze individually rather than in a lump. Strawberries don't freeze well, but most other berries do.

Uncooked strawberry conserve

This has got to be the easiest way to make delicious strawberry conserve, and no cooking means that the fruit still retains its vitamin content.

You will need:

> *1.3 kg (3 lb) firm strawberries*
> *1.8 kg (4 lb) caster sugar*
> *4 tablespoons lemon juice*
> *225 ml (8 fl oz) liquid pectin*

Crush the strawberries into a rough pulp and place into a large glass bowl and stir in the sugar and lemon juice. Leave for about 2 hours until the sugar is completely dissolved into the strawberry juice, stirring occasionally. Gently but thoroughly stir in the pectin, then divide the jam between 225 g (8 oz) jam jars, cover with a lid and leave on a window ledge for up to four days to set. Test with a spoon and, when soft-set, freeze or store in the fridge.

Bottling whole fruits in alcohol

* Choose fruits that are just ripe and unblemished and wash thoroughly. Peel any citrus fruits; hard fruits such as apples should be peeled; stones should be removed from stone fruits.

* Place the prepared fruit in a sterilized Kilner jar, adding spices if desired.

* Make the syrup by pouring the alcohol in a pan and bringing to a boil. Add sugar and stir to dissolve, then remove from heat and leave to cool. Completely cover the fruit in the jar with the cooled syrup mixture and seal.

* Store in a cool dark place for a month so that the flavours can develop before using.

Which fruits work best in alcohol?

* Cherries – preserve in brandy or kirsch and spoon over vanilla ice cream.

* Plums – preserve in port and serve as a side dish with cheese.

* Summer berries – preserve in kirsch and serve with whole berries, whipped cream and crushed meringues.

* Mangoes – preserve with white rum and serve with warm chocolate sauce.

Traditional Rumtopf

'Rum pot' is a traditional German method of preserving fruit in alcohol, and is especially useful when there's a glut of summer berry fruit around. The idea is to layer fruit with sugar and alcohol, adding additional layers to the rumtopf pot as more fruit comes into season. So, you could start with some strawberries and raspberries, for example, sprinkle some sugar between the layers of fruit, then pour on dark rum so that it completely covers the fruit. You could then add cherries, peaches (peeled and quartered), apricots (de-stoned and halved), nectarines (de-stoned and halved), grapes (seedless, sweet), blackberries – whatever soft fruit you have, using more sugar and ensuring that the rum always covers the fruit completely.

Rumtopf fruits can be served hot or cold over ice cream, cakes or flans or with cheese, or simply with whipped cream or crème fraiche. Delicious!

COOK'S TIP

If you're making a rumtopf for a friend, why not make a smaller version in a glass Kilner jar, add the layers, as above, and set it aside for a month so the flavours develop before handing it over?

PICKLES AND CHUTNEYS

Used to enhance the flavours present in a meal, chutneys are usually made using small pieces of vegetables and fruit that are puréed, while in pickles the ingredients are more often left 'chunky' and retain their crunch. The word 'chutney' is said to come from the Hindi word 'chatni', and this flavoursome preserve is thought to have originated in Eastern India during the fifteenth century.

Tomato chutney

Try this easy recipe – it's especially ideal if you have a glut of tomatoes from the garden at the end of the season.
   You will need:

> 1.5 kg (3 lb 5 oz) ripe tomatoes
> 225 g (8 oz) shallots
> 450 g (1 lb) granulated sugar
> 125 g (4½ oz) sultanas
> 1 tablespoon salt
> 1 teaspoon white pepper
> 3 level teaspoons mustard seed
> ½ teaspoon allspice
> 850 ml (1½ pints) vinegar

Skin the tomatoes and roughly chop the shallots. Put all other ingredients into a heavy-based saucepan and bring to a boil. Add the chopped tomatoes and shallots and simmer slowly without a lid until the mixture is thick. Pot into clean glass jars and cover with greaseproof paper. When the chutney has cooled, screw on the jar lid, store and label.

LABELLING YOUR PRESERVES

Always remember to label and date your preserves, as they will keep for at least a year in a cool well-ventilated cupboard – and if there's no label, you'll forget what you have! Also, make decorative labels for pots to give to friends and family. They make great home-made presents – people will marvel at your culinary skills.

INFUSING OIL AND VINEGAR

Flavoured vinegars and oils are useful for dressings, sauces and marinades.

* For herb-flavoured vinegar, try garlic, basil, dill, lavender, rosemary or tarragon.

* Spice your vinegar up with peppercorns, chilli peppers, coriander seeds, mustard or fennel seeds.

* For herb-infused oils, try basil, bay, dill, garlic, mint, oregano, rosemary or thyme.

* Chilli peppers or cumin are among the spices that make tasty companions for good quality oil.

To make herb or spice oil or vinegar

* Take about 60 g (2¼ oz) herb sprigs or whole spices and crush to bring out their flavour.

* Put the herbs or spices into a large jar and cover with 500 ml (18 fl oz) sunflower oil (or extra virgin olive oil) or white wine vinegar.

* Put the lid on the jar and allow it to infuse for 2 to 3 weeks. The flavours will develop more quickly if the jar is placed in the sun.

* Strain the oil or vinegar into bottles and add a sprig of fresh herb or a few fresh spices to each bottle for decoration.

* Close with a cork or plastic-lined cap and label.

*My doctor told me to stop having intimate dinners for four.
Unless there are three other people present.*
ORSON WELLES

Sensational Soups

There's nothing like soup to warm the heart and soul on a cold winter's day. In fact, I like soup all year round – it's comforting and wholesome and just makes me feel better. Here are a few old favourites, all really easy and quick to make.

Borscht

Great colour, great flavour, borscht can be eaten hot or cold and is a staple in Eastern Europe, where each country has its own version.

You will need:

1 large onion, diced
1 carrot, diced
450g (1 lb) raw beetroot, washed (but not peeled)
850ml (1½ pints) vegetable stock
15g (½oz) butter
1 tomato, peeled and chopped
bay leaf
2 teaspoons red wine vinegar
2 teaspoons sugar
freshly ground sea salt
freshly ground black pepper
pinch nutmeg
pinch cinnamon
150ml (5 fl oz) carton soured cream

Place the diced onion and carrot in a large saucepan and add the beetroot, butter and about 600ml (1 pint) of the stock. Bring to a boil and cook for about 1 hour. Add all the remaining ingredients

– except the cream – and cook for another hour. Remove the beetroot from the pan, skin and dice it, then purée the liquid and beetroot together in a food processor. Check the seasoning, reheat the soup and serve, garnished with a swirl of soured cream.

Stilton soup

This begins life as a roux, with the tangy cheese added at the end of the recipe, but whatever way you make it, you couldn't hope for a more warming (and, with the croutons, filling) soup.

You will need:

25g (1 oz) butter
1 onion, finely chopped
25g (1 oz) flour
700 ml (1¼ pints) milk
freshly ground sea salt
freshly ground black pepper
Stilton cheese, crumbled
handful parsley, chopped
garlic croutons

In a large, heavy-based pan, melt the butter and sauté the onion, without browning. Stir in the flour and then gradually add the milk, stirring constantly. Bring to a boil, season to taste and allow to simmer for a few minutes. Just before serving, mix in the crumbled Stilton (about 55–85 g or 2–3 oz should do it, but add cheese to your taste) and chopped parsley. Serve garnished with garlic croutons.

Minestrone

An Italian classic, this very easy version contains bacon, but you can leave it out for a vegetarian version.

You will need:

25 g (1 oz) bacon
1 small leek, washed and finely chopped
1 onion, chopped
small carrot, washed and finely chopped
small turnip, washed and finely chopped
1 stick celery, washed and finely chopped
1 small potato, washed and finely chopped
2 tablespoons peas (fresh or frozen)
700 ml (1¼ pints) vegetable stock
1 small can chopped tomatoes
55 g (2 oz) macaroni or vermicelli
bouquet garni
freshly ground sea salt
freshly ground black pepper
grated Parmesan cheese

Trim any fat off the bacon, cut into very small pieces and fry gently. Soften all the vegetables with the fried bacon for about 8 minutes (or sauté in 25 g/1 oz butter if not using bacon), then add the stock, tomatoes, pasta and bouquet garni, and cook for a further 5 minutes, until the pasta is tender. Season to taste and serve with grated Parmesan.

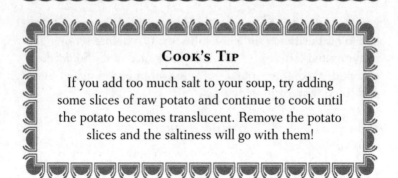

Cook's Tip

If you add too much salt to your soup, try adding some slices of raw potato and continue to cook until the potato becomes translucent. Remove the potato slices and the saltiness will go with them!

Tomato and rice soup

You will need:

450 g (1 lb) ripe tomatoes
1 clove garlic, crushed
2 bay leaves
40 g (1½ oz) butter
2 medium onions, sliced
25 g (1 oz) flour
700 ml (1¼ pints) vegetable stock
1 teaspoon sugar
freshly ground sea salt
freshly ground black pepper
25 g (1 oz) long grain rice

To finish:
2 slices bread
15 g (½ oz) grated cheese
½ teaspoon Dijon mustard

Quarter 350 g (12 oz) of the tomatoes and place in a large saucepan with the crushed garlic, bay leaves and half the butter. Cover and simmer for 10 minutes, then purée in a food processor. Put the onion slices in a large saucepan with the rest of the butter, cover and cook over a very low heat for about 10 to 15 minutes. Remove from the heat and add the flour, stock and puréed tomatoes. Add the sugar and season to taste, then add the rice and simmer for 20 to 30 minutes. Meanwhile, skin the remaining tomatoes, cut into quarters, remove the seeds and shred the flesh. Add to the soup.

To finish, toast the bread on one side, mix together the cheese and mustard and spread on the non-toasted side of the bread. Brown under the grill, cut into fingers and serve with the hot soup. Bliss.

COOK'S TIP

If you make your own meat stock for soups, instead of leaving the stock to cool before removing the solidified fat from the top, try passing two layers of kitchen paper through the stock while it's still hot. This will absorb any fat – and saves time.

Something Sweet

It's no coincidence that if you write the word 'stressed' backwards it spells 'desserts'. Not without reason are these sweet triumphs adored the world over. Dessert, pudding, sweet, call it what you will, this is commonly the final course of the meal, and the word 'dessert' comes from the French *desservir*, meaning 'to clear the table'.

Meringues, fools, ice creams, mousses and good old-fashioned puddings often appear really tricky to make, but don't be put off, there are some really easy recipes that will make you look like the impressive cook you are.

Lemon meringue pie

This is a really simple recipe but the finished article is fantastic. You need to bake the pastry blind before adding the lemon and finishing off with the meringue, but the three stages are straightforward and it's never failed me!

You will need:

1 pack shortcrust pastry

For the lemon mixture:
2 large lemons
425 ml (15 fl oz) water
50 g (1¾ oz) cornfour
225 g (8 oz) caster sugar
3 egg yolks

For the meringue:
115 g (4 oz) caster sugar
3 egg whites

Pre-heat the oven to 160°C/325°F. Following the manufacturer's instructions, roll out the pastry until it is approximately 5 mm in depth (you can check whether you have rolled it enough by laying your 23-cm flan tin on top of the pastry and making sure it will line the base and come up the sides of the tin). Then, using the rolling pin, pick the pastry up and place it in a flan tin. Gently ease the pastry into the tin and press it down at the sides and onto the base. When you have lined the sides and base, cut away any excess pastry and discard.

Cover the pastry in the baking tin with greaseproof paper weighed down with baking beans (or long-grain rice) and bake for about 12 minutes. Then take out the paper and baking beans and return the pastry to the oven for a couple of minutes until it is golden brown. That's the pastry sorted.

For the lemon mixture, first grate the rind off the lemons, and then juice them. Put the cornflour and water in a saucepan and stir together, then add the lemon rind and juice. Stir the mixture over a gentle heat until it is thickening. Separate the eggs and, reserving the egg whites for the meringue, beat the yolks together. Add the yolks to the saucepan and beat the mixture until well combined. When it is thick and very warm (don't boil it!), remove the pan from the heat and allow to cool. When cool, pour the mixture into the baking case. Turn the oven up to 200°C/400°F.

For the meringue, whip the egg whites together in a large bowl or food processor until frothy, then begin to beat in the caster sugar a tablespoon at a time, making sure each spoonful is well combined and the egg whites form stiff, glossy peaks.

Pile the meringue mixture onto the lemon, starting from the outside of the flan dish and working in to the centre. Bake in a hot oven for about 10 minutes, until the meringue is golden brown and hard on the top. Serve warm.

> *Comedy just pokes at problems, rarely confronts them squarely. Drama is like a plate of meat and potatoes, comedy is rather the dessert, a bit like meringue.*
>
> **WOODY ALLEN**

Clafoutis

This easy dessert is a classic French pancake. I usually make mine with cherries, but you could try any soft fruit in season: plums, blackberries, strawberries – whatever you have plenty of. Also, I have made this recipe with bottled cherries out of season and it worked perfectly well.

You will need:

200 g (7 oz) ripe black cherries,
halved and stoned
4 eggs
150 g (5½ oz) sugar
50 g (1¾ oz) flour
300 ml (½ pt) single cream

Pre-heat the oven to 180°C/350°F. Spread the halved and stoned cherries in the bottom of a shallow, ovenproof dish. Whisk together the eggs and sugar, then add the flour, and finally the cream, and pour the mixture over the cherries. Bake for around half an hour, until the 'pancake' has set and is turning golden. Serve lukewarm with a spoon of good vanilla ice cream.

Strawberry ice cream with raspberry coulis

If you have access to lots of summer fruits in season, there really is nothing better than home-made strawberry ice cream. I always thought an ice cream maker was a silly idea, but I soon changed my mind when I was given one. However you can make really good ice cream without one, it just takes a bit longer. The recipe below works both ways. Whichever way you do it, serve with raspberry coulis, delicious cold or heated up (see 'Raspberry sauce' page 145).

You will need:

500 g (1 lb 2 oz) ripe strawberries
100 g (3½ oz) caster sugar
juice of 1 lemon
300 ml (½ pt) double cream

Using a food processor or liquidizer, mash the strawberries, caster sugar and lemon juice and blend to a pulp. You can use the pulp or push the strawberry mixture through a sieve to remove the seeds. Place in the fridge to chill. Whip the cream into soft peaks and fold into the chilled strawberry mixture.

If making by hand, pour the mixture into a suitable clean plastic container and freeze for 2 hours. After 2 hours, take the mixture out and put it in the food processor again to break up the ice crystals, and repeat this process twice more: back in the freezer for 2 hours, break up the crystals, back in the freezer, break up the crystals.

If using an ice cream maker, turn the mixture into the machine and churn and freeze as per the manufacturer's instructions.

COOK'S TIP

When making ice cream, adding alcohol
to a fruit purée slows down the freezing process,
so add with care!

Chocolate mousse

I hate fiddling about with gelatine, which is why this easy chocolate mousse is my favourite. This recipe will make enough for six people.

You will need:

450 g (1 lb) good dark chocolate
(at least 70 per cent cocoa solids)
100 g (3½ oz) caster sugar
2 tablespoons butter
6 eggs, separated

Melt the chocolate in a bowl over hot water then combine it with the caster sugar and butter. Allow this mixture to cool before adding the egg yolks and blend in well. Whisk the 6 egg whites until they turn white and hold their shape, then fold them carefully – and a little at a time at first – into the chocolate mixture. Cover the bowl and chill for at least four hours before serving.

Blueberry fool

A fantastic summer dessert, you can use raspberries, strawberries – any seasonal fruit in this easy no-cook recipe.

225 g (8 oz) fresh blueberries
50 g (1¾ oz) caster sugar
150 ml (5 fl oz) double cream
150 ml (5 fl oz) plain yogurt

In a large bowl, crush the blueberries with a fork, add the sugar and leave to stand for 10 minutes or so. Beat the cream until thick then, very gradually, add the yogurt, blending it into the cream. Add the blueberry mixture but try not to stir it in too thoroughly – go for a 'marbled' effect. Pour into serving dishes and refrigerate for a couple of hours before serving.

> *Seize the moment. Remember all those women on the* TITANIC *who waved off the dessert cart.*
>
> **ERMA BOMBECK**

Sweet Sauces and Custard

Sauces can transform the most mundane ice cream dessert or put the magic back into a steamed pud. All the sauces here are easy and quick to make. The sabayon does take some mastering, but once you've got it, you can use the basic recipe and experiment with your own flavours.

Sabayon sauce

This is the French version of the Italian favourite Zabaglione, and is usually served warm as an accompaniment to fresh soft fruits, fruit compotes or even steamed puddings.

You will need:

> 3 egg yolks
> 25g (1oz) caster sugar
> 50ml (2 floz) dessert wine
> 1 tablespoon Madeira or sweet sherry

Whisk the egg yolks and sugar together in a heatproof bowl until they are foamy and pale. Set the bowl over a pan of simmering water and, whisking constantly, add the dessert wine a little at a time, until the mixture begins to thicken. Continue whisking until the mixture is thick enough to leave a ribbon trail. Finally, add the Madeira or sherry. Serve immediately.

Flavour your sabayon with

* the juice of one lemon, or

* the juice of half an orange

Raspberry sauce

No one would refuse ice cream when accompanied by this sauce! You can use frozen raspberries if the fruit's out of season.
You will need:

> 450g (1 lb) fresh raspberries
> 2 tablespoons lemon juice
> 2 tablespoons icing sugar

Place all the ingredients into a food processor or blender and whiz together until smooth. Pass the mixture through a sieve, discarding the pulp. Keep in the fridge until ready to use.

Butterscotch sauce

This is a sweet and warming pouring sauce – perfect over ice cream as well as hot desserts.
You will need:

> 85g (3oz) butter
> 175g (6oz) brown sugar
> 2 tablespoons golden syrup
> 85ml (3 floz) double cream

Melt the butter in a small saucepan over a low heat and stir in the sugar and golden syrup. When the sugar has dissolved, add the cream and bring to a boil. Remove from the heat and allow it to cool slightly before serving.

Brandy butter

Where would a Christmas pudding be without brandy butter? Simple but classic, this melting mixture is a perfect accompaniment to many hot desserts.

You will need:

> *175g (6oz) unsalted butter*
> *50g (1¾oz) icing sugar*
> *3 tablespoons brandy*

In a small bowl, cream the butter and sugar together, then add the brandy and beat together until smooth. Place in the fridge until needed.

Chocolate sauce

This one speaks for itself . . . it's important to use good chocolate, though, as it's the cocoa solids content that dictates the amount of flavour the chocolate has.

You will need:

> *125g (4½oz) dark chocolate*
> *(at least 70 per cent cocoa solids)*
> *150ml (5 floz) double cream*
> *150ml (5 floz) milk*
> *1 tablespoon caster sugar*

Put all the ingredients into a medium-sized, heavy-based saucepan and stir together constantly over a low heat until the mixture is fully melted and smooth.

Home-made custard

Warming and delicious, proper home-made custard is nothing like the stuff we used to get at school.

You will need:

2 vanilla pods
600 ml (1 pint) milk
6 egg yolks
50 g (1¾ oz) granulated sugar

Split the vanilla pods lengthways and scrape out the seeds, reserving both. Bring the milk almost to a boil, remove from the heat and add the vanilla pods and seeds, leaving it to stand for 15 minutes to allow the vanilla to infuse the milk. In a large bowl, whisk the egg yolks and sugar together until the mixture is thick and creamy. Remove the vanilla from the milk, then begin to stir it into the egg mixture. Return the custard mixture into a large, heavy-based saucepan and cook over a low heat, stirring constantly, until the custard thickens. Serve hot or cold.

Cakes and Biscuits

CAKES

I've always wanted to be a cake maker, but try as I might I'm just not good at sponges – but I have learned a few tricks on the way. Most of the cakes in our house are baked by my husband, who obviously has the right touch.

Perfect Victoria Sandwich

This might sound like a boring recipe but if you can crack this one you can bake any cake.

You will need:

> *225g (8oz) self-raising flour*
> *pinch of salt*
> *225g (8oz) butter, softened*
> *225g (8oz) caster sugar*
> *4 eggs, lightly beaten*
> *4 tablespoons strawberry jam*

Preheat the oven to 190°C/375°F. Lightly grease two 20-cm round cake tins, then sprinkle in a light coating of plain flour and shake the tins to coat them evenly, then turn the tins over to get rid of any excess flour. Sift the flour and salt together. Put the butter and sugar in a large bowl and, using a wooden spoon, cream them together until the mixture is light and fluffy. Add the eggs a little at a time, beating the mixture together well after each addition. Then, using a metal spoon, gently fold in the sifted flour, using a 'figure of eight' movement to keep as much air in the mixture as possible. Spoon the mixture into the prepared baking tins and bake for about 25 minutes, when the tops should be golden. Turn out to cool on a rack, then spread on the jam and sandwich the cakes together.

Portuguese Custard Tarts

These are fantastic little cakes that taste like heaven and are easy as the proverbial pie. This makes 16 cakes and you need muffin tins in which to bake them.

You will need:

> *1 packet puff pastry*
> *175g (6oz) granulated sugar*
> *250ml (9 floz) milk*
> *seeds from 1 vanilla pod*
> *3 tablespoons cornflour*
> *6 egg yolks, beaten*

Preheat the oven to 180°C/350°F. Lightly grease the muffin tins. Cut the puff pastry into 4 pieces and roll each piece out until it is about 3mm thick, then cut each piece into 4 again and use the 16 pieces to line the muffin tins. Place the tins in the fridge to chill. Heat the sugar, milk and vanilla seeds in a saucepan and turn up the heat. When hot, take 3 tablespoons of the mixture from the pan and blend together with the cornflour to create a smooth paste. Add the paste to the milk and heat gently, stirring constantly, until the mixture thickens. Remove from the heat and stir in the egg yolks. Then pour the mixture into the pastry cases and bake for about 20 minutes, or until the filling is lightly browning on top and the pastry crust is golden.

COOK'S TIPS

In my search for sponge perfection there are a few tricks I've learned that might help you perfect your technique.

* Use softened (not melted) butter for easier blending.

* Make sure your eggs are at room temperature when you beat them in.

* Make sure the oven is preheated to the proper temperature before you put the cake mixture in.

* Before you put the cake tin in the oven, get rid of any potential air bubbles by tapping the tin gently on the work surface.

* Bake cakes in the centre of the oven, and if you are baking a big batch, switch the cakes round halfway through the cooking so they cook evenly.

* Don't be tempted to open the oven door before 15 minutes' cooking is up.

Mrs Dixon's Rich Fruit Cake

My mother-in-law gave me this recipe – along with countless others and many of the Cook's Tips, come to that! She is renowned as an ace cake maker. This one should be made well ahead, as it improves with storing.

You will need:

900 g (2 lb) mixed dried fruit and peel
175 ml (6 fl oz) brandy
4 large eggs
225 g (8 oz) butter, softened
225 g (8 oz) dark brown sugar
1 tablespoon black treacle
350 g (12 oz) plain white flour
1 heaped tsp ground cinnamon
½ teaspoon salt
115 g (4 oz) ground almonds
225 g (8 oz) glacé cherries

On the day before baking, soak the mixed, dried fruit in 8 tablespoons of the brandy. Preheat the oven to 160°C/325°F. In a small bowl, whisk the remaining brandy with the eggs. In a large bowl, cream the softened butter with the brown sugar and treacle. Sift together the flour, cinnamon and salt, and add a spoonful to the creamed mixture to prevent curdling, then add a little of the egg mixture, then more of the flour, more of the egg, adding more of each alternately until both are used up. Stir in the ground almonds, the soaked fruit and the glacé cherries. By this time the mixture should be stiff. Spoon the mixture into a greased and lined 20-cm square cake tin and bake for 1½ hours, then turn the oven down to 150°C/300°F and bake for a further 2 hours, by which time a skewer inserted into the middle of the cake should come out clean. Leave the cake to cool in the tin, then remove and wrap well or store in an airtight container. For an extra-moist cake, prick with a skewer and pour over two or three tablespoons of brandy before storing.

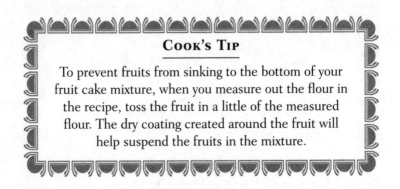

COOK'S TIP

To prevent fruits from sinking to the bottom of your fruit cake mixture, when you measure out the flour in the recipe, toss the fruit in a little of the measured flour. The dry coating created around the fruit will help suspend the fruits in the mixture.

Florentines

These always look good on the plate and are very easy to make. This recipe will make about 30 cakes.

You will need:

115g (4oz) butter
85g (3oz) caster sugar
1 tablespoon double cream
115g (4oz) flaked almonds
55g (2oz) chopped candied peel
55g (2oz) glacé cherries, chopped
175g (6oz) good, plain chocolate

Preheat the oven to 180°C/350°F. Melt the butter in a saucepan over a gentle heat, then add the sugar. Continue to heat gently, stirring constantly, until the sugar dissolves. Add the cream and bring the mixture to a boil. Still stirring, let it bubble gently for a minute. Add the almonds, peel and cherries and mix together well. Using two spoons, put small amounts of the mixture onto baking trays lined with baking parchment. Leave plenty of space between each cake to allow them to spread. Bake for around 8 minutes until just golden, then remove from the oven and, using a spatula, shape the Florentines into neater rounds. Allow to cool. Meanwhile, melt the chocolate in a bowl over a pan of simmering water. When the Florentines are cool, spread the bottom of each one with the melted chocolate and allow to set on the baking parchment.

BISCUITS

There are two main types of biscuit – dropped and rolled. Dropped biscuits have a less firm dough than rolled, and can literally be dropped from a spoon or piped onto the baking sheet and put in the oven. Rolled biscuits have a firmer dough that is rolled flat and cut out or rolled into a sausage shape and sliced. You can add all sorts of flavours into these two basic recipes – try using a tablespoon of dried lavender flowers or some chopped mixed nuts in the dropped biscuit method, or some chopped glacé cherries or finely grated citrus peel when you fancy rolling the biscuits.

Basic recipe for dropped biscuits

You will need:

> 125 g (4½ oz) *butter (unsalted)*
> 150 g (5½ oz) *caster sugar*
> 2 *egg whites*
> 100 g (3½ oz) *plain flour*
> 125 g (4½ oz) *ground almonds*

Preheat the oven to 180°C/350°F. Melt the butter and add the caster sugar. When the mixture has cooled, blend in the egg whites, followed by the flour, then the almonds. Make sure the dough is well combined, then take about a teaspoonful of the dough and drop it onto the baking sheet. Try to ensure that the shapes are about the same size so that they bake evenly, and spread them well apart so they have space to spread as necessary. Bake for about 15 minutes.

Basic recipe for rolled biscuits

You will need:

125g (4½oz) butter (unsalted), softened
150g (5½oz) caster sugar
2 egg yolks
225g (8oz) plain flour
50g (1¾oz) currants (or sultanas)

Preheat the oven to 190°C/375°F. Cream together the softened butter with the caster sugar and, when smooth, beat in the egg yolks, flour and fruit. Knead the dough until it works together, then chill it in the fridge for an hour. When it's chilled, either roll the dough out with a rolling pin and cut the biscuits out with biscuit cutters, or roll the dough into a sausage shape and cut into even slices. Arrange on a baking sheet and bake for about 15 minutes.

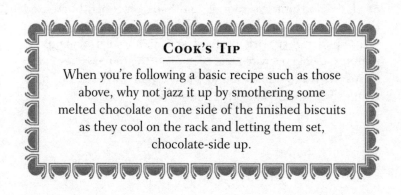

Cook's Tip

When you're following a basic recipe such as those above, why not jazz it up by smothering some melted chocolate on one side of the finished biscuits as they cool on the rack and letting them set, chocolate-side up.

Petticoat Tails

My favourite biscuit (though technically it might be better called a cake), a proper Scottish shortbread that tastes good and reminds me of afternoon tea at my grandma's.

You will need:

450 g (1 lb) plain flour
225 g (8 oz) butter, softened
175 g (6 oz) caster sugar
water as required

Preheat the oven to 180°C/350°F. Sift the flour into a large bowl and rub in the butter. When the flour and butter are well rubbed together, stir in the sugar and enough water to make a smooth dough. Divide the dough into 2 equal portions and roll each portion into 2 round 'cakes' the size of a dinner plate. Using a 7-cm round pastry cutter, cut out the middle of each cake and reserve. Carefully divide the ring of cake left into 8 equal portions, and put the rounds and 'tails' on a lightly greased baking sheet covered with greaseproof paper, placing them a little apart. Dust with caster sugar and bake for about 20 minutes. Cool on a wire rack, then place the round cakes in the centre with the 'tails' around them. Dust with a little more caster sugar and serve with a pot of tea.

Measurement Charts

OVEN TEMPERATURES

Celsius	Fahrenheit	Gas	Description
110ºC	225ºF	¼	Cool
120ºC	250ºF	½	Cool
140ºC	275ºF	1	Very low
150ºC	300ºF	2	Very low
160ºC	325ºF	3	Low
170ºC	325ºF	3	Moderate
180ºC	350ºF	4	Moderate
190ºC	375ºF	5	Moderately hot
200ºC	400ºF	6	Hot
220ºC	425ºC	7	Hot
230ºC	450ºF	8	Very hot

US CUPS

Cups	Metric
¼ cup	60 ml
⅓ cup	70 ml
½ cup	125 ml
⅔ cup	150 ml
¾ cup	175 ml
1 cup	250 ml
1½ cups	375 ml
2 cups	500 ml
3 cups	750 ml
4 cups	1 litre
6 cups	1.5 litres

SPOONS

Metric	Imperial
1.25 ml	¼ teaspoon
2.5 ml	½ teaspoon
5 ml	1 teaspoon
10 ml	2 teaspoons
15 ml	3 teaspoons/1 tablespoon
30 ml	2 tablespoons
45 ml	3 tablespoons
60 ml	4 tablespoons
75 ml	5 tablespoons
90 ml	6 tablespoons

VOLUME		WEIGHT			
Metric	**Imperial**	**Metric**	**Imperial**	**Metric**	**Imperial**
25 ml	1 fl oz	5 g	⅛ oz	325 g	11½ oz
50 ml	2 fl oz	10 g	¼ oz	350 g	12 oz
75 ml	2½ fl oz	15 g	½ oz	375 g	13 oz
100 ml	3½ fl oz	20 g	¾ oz	400 g	14 oz
125 ml	4 fl oz	25 g	1 oz	425 g	15 oz
150 ml	5 fl oz/¼ pint	35 g	1¼ oz	450 g	1 lb
175 ml	6 fl oz	40 g	1½ oz	500 g	1 lb 2 oz
200 ml	7 fl oz/⅓ pint	50 g	1¾ oz	550 g	1 lb 4 oz
225 ml	8 fl oz	55 g	2 oz	600 g	1 lb 5 oz
250 ml	9 fl oz	60 g	2¼ oz	650 g	1 lb 7 oz
300 ml	10 fl oz/½ pint	70 g	2½ oz	700 g	1 lb 9 oz
350 ml	12 fl oz	75 g	2¾ oz	750 g	1 lb 10 oz
400 ml	14 fl oz	85 g	3 oz	800 g	1 lb 12 oz
425 ml	15 fl oz/¾ pint	90 g	3¼ oz	850 g	1 lb 14 oz
450 ml	16 fl oz	100 g	3½ oz	900 g	2 lb
500 ml	18 fl oz	115 g	4 oz	950 g	2 lb 2 oz
568 ml	20 fl oz/1 pint	125 g	4½ oz	1 kg	2 lb 4 oz
600 ml	1 pint milk	140 g	5 oz	1.25 kg	2 lb 12 oz
700 ml	1¼ pints	150 g	5½ oz	1.3 kg	3 lb
850 ml	1½ pints	175 g	6 oz	1.5 kg	3 lb 5 oz
1 litre	1¾ pints	200 g	7 oz	1.6 kg	3 lb 8 oz
1.2 litres	2 pints	225 g	8 oz	1.8 kg	4 lb
1.3 litres	2¼ pints	250 g	9 oz	2 kg	4 lb 8 oz
1.4 litres	2½ pints	275 g	9¾ oz	2.25 kg	5 lb
1.5 litres	2¾ pints	280 g	10 oz	2.5 kg	5 lb 8 oz
1.7 litres	3 pints	300 g	10½ oz	2.7 kg	6 lb
2 litres	3½ pints	315 g	11 oz	3 kg	6 lb 8 oz
2.5 litres	4½ pints				
2.8 litres	5 pints				
3 litres	5¼ pints				

Also available in this bestselling series:

The Boys' Book:
How To Be The Best At Everything
ISBN: 978-1-905158-64-5   Price: £7.99

The Girls' Book:
How To Be The Best At Everything
ISBN: 978-1-905158-79-9   Price: £7.99

The Mums' Book:
For The Mum Who's Best At Everything
ISBN: 978-1-84317-246-8   Price: £9.99

The Dads' Book:
For The Dad Who's Best At Everything
ISBN: 978-1-84317-250-5   Price: £9.99

The Grannies' Book:
For The Granny Who's Best At Everything
ISBN: 978-1-84317-251-2   Price: £9.99

The Grandads' Book:
For The Grandad Who's Best At Everything
ISBN 978-1-84317-308-3   Price: £9.99

The Gardeners' Book:
For The Gardener Who's Best At Everything
ISBN 978-1-84317-327-4   Price: £9.99

The Lovers' Book:
For The Lover Who's Best At Everything
ISBN: 978-1-84317-285-7   Price: £9.99

The Wives' Book:
For The Wife Who's Best At Everything
ISBN 978-1-84317-325-0   Price: £9.99

The Husbands' Book:
For The Husband Who's Best At Everything
ISBN 978-1-84317-326-7   Price: £9.99

The Family Book:
Amazing Things To Do Together
ISBN: 978-1-906082-10-9   Price £14.99

The Christmas Book:
How To Have The Best Christmas Ever
ISBN: 978-1-84317-282-6   Price: £9.99

These titles and all other Michael O'Mara Books
are available by post from:
Bookpost Ltd
PO Box 29, Douglas, Isle of Man IM99 1BQ

To pay by credit card, use the following contact details:

Telephone: **01624 677237** / Fax: **01624 670923**
Email: **bookshop@enterprise.net**
Internet: **www.bookpost.co.uk**

Postage and packing is free in the UK;
overseas customers should allow £5 per hardback book.